OECD Development Co-operation Peer Reviews: New Zealand 2015

Please cite this publication as:
OECD (2015), *OECD Development Co-operation Peer Reviews: New Zealand 2015*, OECD Development Co-operation Peer Reviews, OECD Publishing, Paris.
http://dx.doi.org/10.1787/9789264235588-en

ISBN 978-92-64-23557-1 (print)
ISBN 978-92-64-23558-8 (PDF)

Series: OECD Development Co-operation Peer Reviews
ISSN 2309-7124 (print)
ISSN 2309-7132 (online)

Corrigenda to OECD publications may be found on line at: *www.oecd.org/about/publishing/corrigenda.htm*.

Conducting the peer review

The OECD's Development Assistance Committee (DAC) conducts periodic reviews of the individual development co-operation efforts of DAC members. The policies and programmes of each member are critically examined approximately once every four or five years. Five members are examined annually. The OECD's Development Co-operation Directorate provides analytical support, and develops and maintains, in close consultation with the Committee, the methodology and analytical framework – known as the Reference Guide – within which the peer reviews are undertaken.

The objectives of DAC peer reviews are to improve the quality and effectiveness of development co-operation policies and systems, and to promote good development partnerships for better impact on poverty reduction and sustainable development in developing countries. DAC peer reviews assess the performance of a given member, not just that of its development co-operation agency, and examine both policy and implementation. They take an integrated, system-wide perspective on the development co-operation and humanitarian assistance activities of the member under review.

The peer review is prepared by a team, consisting of representatives of the Secretariat working with officials from two DAC members who are designated as "examiners". The country under review provides a memorandum setting out the main developments in its policies and programmes. Then the Secretariat and the examiners visit the capital to interview officials, parliamentarians, as well as civil society and NGO representatives of the donor country to obtain a first-hand insight into current issues surrounding the development co-operation efforts of the member concerned. Field visits assess how members are implementing the major DAC policies, principles and concerns, and review operations in recipient countries, particularly with regard to poverty reduction, sustainability, gender equality and other aspects of participatory development, and local aid co-ordination. During the field visit, the team meets with representatives of the partner country's administration, parliamentarians, civil society and other development partners.

The Secretariat then prepares a draft report on the member's development co-operation which is the basis for the DAC review meeting at the OECD. At this meeting senior officials from the member under review respond to questions formulated by the Committee in association with the examiners.

This review contains the Main Findings and Recommendations of the Development Assistance Committee and the report of the Secretariat. It was prepared with examiners from Ireland and Norway for the Peer Review of New Zealand on 20 May 2015.

The New Zealand peer review was undertaken in parallel with a Pacific Forum Compact Development Partner Review of New Zealand. The respective review teams conducted a number of joint sessions during their work in Wellington and in Kiribati and participated in joint feedback sessions.

Table of contents

Tables

Figures

Boxes

Abbreviations and acronyms

ADB	Asian Development Bank
ASEAN	Association of Southeast Asian Nations
CID	Council for International Development
CPA	Country programmable aid
CSO	Civil society organisation
DAC	Development Assistance Committee
FAP	Forward Aid Plan
GDP	Gross domestic product
GNI	Gross national income
IDA	International Development Association
IDG	International Development Group
LDC	Least developed country
MDG	Millennium Development Goal
MFAT	Ministry of Foreign Affairs and Trade
NGO	Non-governmental organisation
NZECO	New Zealand Export Credit Office
ODA	Official development assistance
PACER Plus	The Pacific Agreement on Closer Economic Relations
PIF	Pacific Islands Forum Compact
PCD	Policy coherence for development
RSE	Recognised Seasonal Employer Scheme
SIDS	Small island developing states
UNFCCC	United Nations Framework Convention on Climate Change

Signs used:

EUR	Euro
USD	United States dollars
NZD	New Zealand dollars
( )	Secretariat estimate in whole or part
-	(Nil)
0.0	Negligible
..	Not available
...	Not available separately, but included in total
n.a.	Not applicable

Slight discrepancies in totals are due to rounding.

Annual average exchange rate: 1 NZD = USD

2009	2010	2011	2012	2013
1.5988	1.3876	1.2664	1.2349	1.2203

New Zealand's aid at a glance

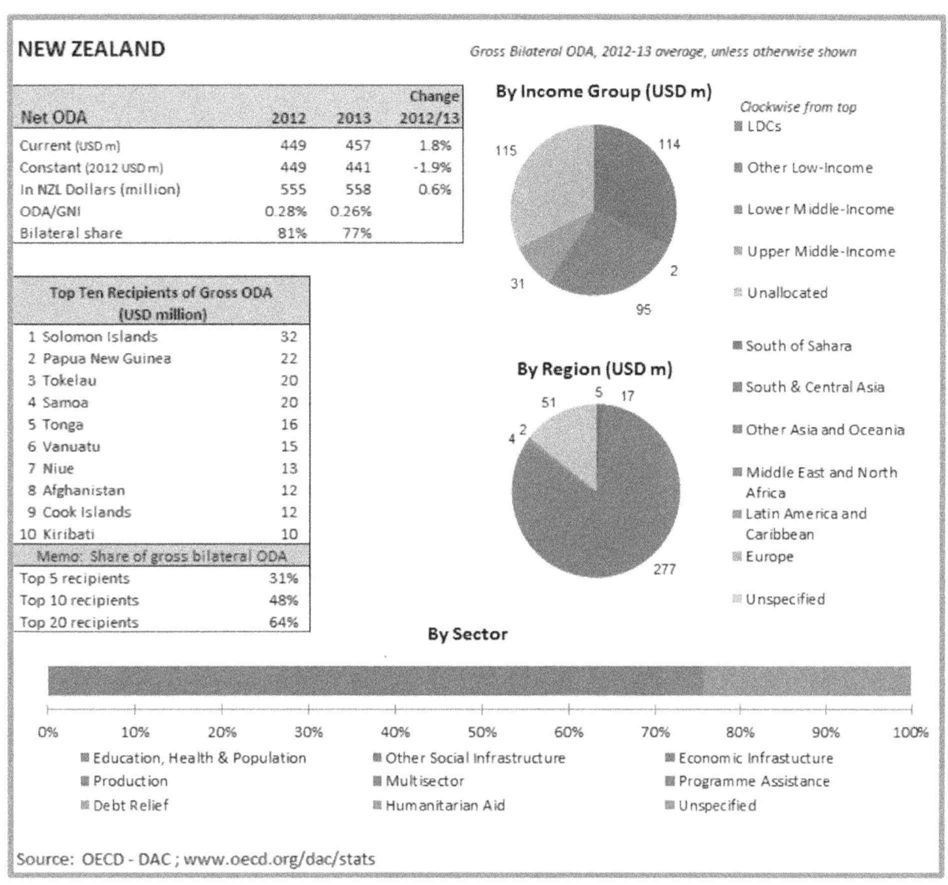

NEW ZEALAND

Gross Bilateral ODA, 2012-13 average, unless otherwise shown

Net ODA	2012	2013	Change 2012/13
Current (USD m)	449	457	1.8%
Constant (2012 USD m)	449	441	-1.9%
In NZL Dollars (million)	555	558	0.6%
ODA/GNI	0.28%	0.26%	
Bilateral share	81%	77%	

Top Ten Recipients of Gross ODA (USD million)	
1 Solomon Islands	32
2 Papua New Guinea	22
3 Tokelau	20
4 Samoa	20
5 Tonga	16
6 Vanuatu	15
7 Niue	13
8 Afghanistan	12
9 Cook Islands	12
10 Kiribati	10
Memo: Share of gross bilateral ODA	
Top 5 recipients	31%
Top 10 recipients	48%
Top 20 recipients	64%

Source: OECD - DAC ; www.oecd.org/dac/stats

Figure 0.1 New Zealand's implementation of 2010 peer review recommendations

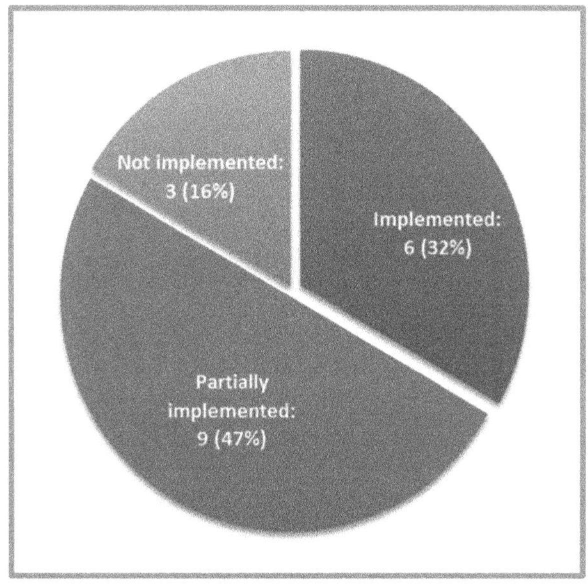

Context of the New Zealand peer review

Political and economic context

New Zealand held a general election in September 2014. The National Party won 47% of the party vote. They negotiated formal support agreements for the incoming parliament with the Māori Party, United Future and Act parties, to enter into government. John Key remained prime minister for a third term. Murray McCully remained the Minister of Foreign Affairs.

In October 2014, New Zealand won one of five non-permanent seats on the United Nations Security Council. Their two-year mandate started in January 2015.

In 2014, the population of New Zealand was 4.5 million and gross domestic product (GDP) per capita at purchasing power parity exchange rates was USD 35 968.

The New Zealand economy has performed well in recent years. Average economic growth in 2014 was just over 3%, similar to the rates recorded over the past three years. The expansion has mainly been driven by a large increase in the terms of trade, construction activity in Canterbury and Auckland and high levels of net immigration. In per capita terms, real GDP reached the pre-recession peak in the second quarter of 2012 and by the fourth quarter of 2014 had increased a further 4.4%.

The post-crisis increase in unemployment has been partly reversed (5.7% according to latest data), and inflation remains low. Aided by the increase in farm export volumes, tourism receipts, the terms of trade and reinsurance pay-outs related to the Canterbury earthquakes, the current account deficit has fallen from a peak of 7.3% of GDP in 2008 to 3.3% of GDP in 2014.

Considerable progress has been made in reducing the central government budget deficit, which had increased markedly during the recession and following the earthquakes, with a small surplus projected for the fiscal year to June 2016.

Reference: OECD (forthcoming), *OECD Economic Surveys: New Zealand 2015*, OECD Publishing, Paris; OECD (2015), "New Zealand", OECD Data (dataset), http://data.oecd.org/new-zealand.htm (accessed on 18 March 2015).

The DAC's main findings and recommendations

1 Towards a comprehensive New Zealand development effort

Indicator: The member has a broad, strategic approach to development and financing for development beyond aid. This is reflected in overall policies, co-ordination within its government system, and operations

Main Findings

New Zealand is widely considered to be a "good global citizen". This reputation is partly related to its development friendly approach, for example in trade and climate negotiations. New Zealand advocates consistently for its neighbours in the Pacific region and for small island developing states more broadly, many of which are among the most vulnerable countries on Earth. Its "Pacific focus, global reach" outlook represents a strategic approach to development for New Zealand.

As a supporter of small island developing states New Zealand has, for example, advocated in its own region and internationally for the right of states to protect and sustainably manage their ocean resources, in particular their fisheries. New Zealand's successful election to a non-permanent seat at the United Nations Security Council in 2014 presents it with further opportunities to demonstrate global leadership on priority issues with clear development benefits, such as conflict prevention, peacekeeping and environmental security.

In line with this strategic approach, New Zealand has made a demonstrable effort to secure development benefits from policies beyond official development assistance (ODA). A liberal trading system, employment schemes, and lower remittance costs are a few examples of policies that go beyond aid to impact positively on development, particularly in the Pacific region.

A commitment to policy coherence for sustainable development is stated in policy. Alignment of foreign, trade and development aims and influence is facilitated by the re-integration of the development programme into the Ministry of Foreign Affairs and Trade. The International Development Group, within the ministry, also builds strategic relationships with other parts of the New Zealand government through long-term partnership arrangements. It is encouraging, and necessary, that the next generation of partnership arrangements will locate whole-of-government relationships and support in a broader policy coherence perspective.

In terms of development finance, besides remittances (USD 1.3 billion in 2012), ODA is by far the largest resource flow from New Zealand to developing countries. However, like many DAC members, New Zealand increasingly looks to use ODA to partner with the private sector and leverage private investments. The 2013 Pacific Energy Summit is an example of success in using this approach.

New Zealand can now look to build on these achievements and identify options for making further progress.

Firstly, New Zealand can raise the ambition of its policy coherence for sustainable development agenda. This would be in line with the expanded and universal agenda of the Sustainable Development Goals from 2015. New Zealand can seek further development impact from a range of non-ODA policies. Establishing policy coherence for sustainable development objectives beyond short-term, annual planning cycles is likely to increase their development benefits. Introducing measures of success is likely to improve the government's ability to monitor and track those development benefits.

Secondly, on financing, the ministry could start tracking flows of finance beyond ODA, in the spirit of the new statistical measure being designed by the OECD's Development Assistance Committee (DAC) to capture total official support for sustainable development.

Finally, New Zealand should be clear on its private sector objectives, and means of delivering them, given the challenging environment for private sector engagement in the region.

Recommendation

1.1 To support its commitment to the Sustainable Development Goals, New Zealand should establish a prioritised, medium to long-term agenda to further promote policy coherence in areas with potential development benefit.

2 New Zealand's vision and policies for development co-operation

Indicator: Clear political directives, policies and strategies shape the member's development co-operation and are in line with international commitments and guidance

Main findings

New Zealand has set out a clear vision for its aid programme. The purpose is to "support sustainable development in developing countries, in order to reduce poverty and to contribute to a more secure, equitable and prosperous world."

The programme is directed by a hierarchy of policies and strategies, and guided by a series of plans, frameworks and commitments. The priorities are focused, and build on a clear rationale in terms of New Zealand's comparative advantage. Policies and strategies contain a strong commitment to the principles of effective development co-operation.

This clarity of purpose enables the strategic and consistent use of ODA funding. For example, New Zealand's policies and strategies, since 2011, have consistently increased New Zealand's thematic focus on sustainable economic development and geographic focus on the Pacific region. New Zealand is also transferring its experience in the Pacific to small islands in the Caribbean, Atlantic and Indian Ocean regions. Finally, focus and scale are also being achieved by having more larger and longer-term activities in the portfolio, with its "five plus" agenda (programming at least five years and over NZD 5 million).

While, there is no specialised policy for New Zealand's development co-operation in fragile states, New Zealand has signed the New Deal for Engagement in Fragile States. New Zealand's guidelines for applying aid effectiveness in fragile states draws on the New Deal principles, and provide a useful guide on how to apply them in practice.

Another example of clear strategy is in relation to multilateral organisations. New Zealand sets out the rationale for engagement with multilateral agencies, including the rationale for funding and the outcomes it seeks. New Zealand takes a focused and consistent approach, aligning its multilateral priorities with its own geographic and sectoral focus. In line with its Pacific focus, for example, New Zealand seeks to leverage multilateral resources for the benefit of the region and often acts as a broker for multilateral development banks in Pacific countries. In line with best practice, New Zealand draws on multilateral organisations' own accountability structures, complemented by other donor performance assessments, rather than conducting their own assessments. New Zealand actively seeks to support improvements across the multilateral system and does not impose additional reporting requirements.

Therefore, the overall vision and strategy of New Zealand's development co-operation is clear. There are, however, aspects of its own policy where New Zealand could show a clearer commitment to implementation: a focus on fighting poverty and on integrating cross-cutting issues.

New Zealand works in environments that are vulnerable, high risk, disaster-prone and fragile, if not always low income. New Zealand adapts its approaches to different country contexts. However, it is not clear how a policy commitment to reducing poverty translates into the design, monitoring and evaluation of country strategies and programming. New Zealand needs to be able to demonstrate that its increasing focus on the drivers and enablers of economic growth translates into lifting people out of poverty.

The International Development Group's stated ambition is to effectively integrate cross-cutting issues, including gender equality, human rights and environmental sustainability, into all policies, programmes and activities. A three-year strategy on cross-cutting issues was put in place in 2012 to build staff capability, to integrate these issues into business processes, to reinforce leadership and accountability, to manage specific activities and to strengthen policy advice. There is limited evidence to suggest that this strategy has improved the integration of cross-cutting issues into all aspects of New Zealand's development co-operation.

Recommendations

2.1 To demonstrate that New Zealand's programming makes a positive difference to the lives of poor and vulnerable people in its partner countries, as intended by its policy commitments, New Zealand should develop policy guidance, and promote monitoring and evaluation of poverty impacts.

2.2 To meet its commitment to mainstream the cross-cutting issues of environmental sustainability, gender equality and human rights, New Zealand should continue to focus on developing staff capability and management accountability in these areas.

3 Allocating New Zealand's official development assistance

Indicator: The member's international and national commitments drive aid volume and allocations

Main findings

New Zealand's progress towards meeting domestic and international ODA targets has been affected by the Christchurch earthquakes and the global financial crisis. Given these shocks, New Zealand is to be commended for the increase it was able to make in ODA spending between 2010 and 2012.

ODA currently stands at USD 502 million (provisional 2014 figures), equivalent to 0.27% of gross national income (GNI). This is well below the 0.7% commitment and below the average of 0.39% for DAC members. New Zealand's performance against this target, which has not exceeded 0.3% in recent years, does not compare well with countries of a similar size, economy and population.

With its economy recovering well, New Zealand now has an opportunity to set more ambitious projections for overall ODA volume. As New Zealand moves towards budget surplus, reviewing forward spending plans will help it set out a path towards meeting its international commitment to total ODA/GNI, which will be especially important looking ahead to the 2015 agreements on financing for development and the global Sustainable Development Goals.

New Zealand's allocations to least developed countries (LDCs) have to be viewed in light of its focus on the Pacific, which – while including many non-LDCs – also includes many countries internationally recognised as vulnerable and in need because of their status as small island developing states. Several of New Zealand's priority countries have graduated out of LDC status, and several more will over the coming years. New Zealand should, however, increasingly focus its non-Pacific, non-small island programme on LDCs in order for it to make progress towards the LDC target.

Notwithstanding the lack of progress on the total ODA commitment, bilateral and multilateral ODA allocations are consistent with New Zealand's strategic priorities, as the rest of this section illustrates.

New Zealand forecasted approximately 57% of bilateral ODA to be disbursed to the Pacific region between 2012/13 and 2014/15. During the same period, New Zealand set a target of 40% of sector allocable aid for sectors under the sustainable economic development theme, which it is likely to exceed. These sectors include transport, energy, and agriculture and fisheries.

New Zealand has 15 priority partner countries, 12 in the Pacific and 3 in Asia, all of which are among its top 20 ODA recipients. The number of priority countries has reduced from 17 at the time of the last peer review due to the shift to regional programming in Southeast Asia. In relation to the 2012-13 average, New Zealand has a slightly lower concentration compared to the DAC country average in the top 5 and 10 countries, but higher in the top 15 and 20 countries.

In 2013, New Zealand programmed 69% of bilateral ODA at partner country level. New Zealand's share of country programmable aid was well above the DAC country average (54.5%). This means more of New Zealand's resources are being programmed in-country, which has potential benefits for its quality and effectiveness. Further, New Zealand is providing a good level of predictability and transparency to partner countries thanks to its forward-looking spending plans.

It is also notable that project-type interventions, although the largest share of New Zealand's country programmable aid, are well below the total DAC share of gross disbursement. New Zealand's share of budget support, on the other hand, was well above the total DAC share in 2012 and has been increasing since 2011, in contrast to most DAC members.

In 2013, New Zealand allocated 23% of total ODA as core contributions to multilateral organisations. It channelled a further 6% of its bilateral ODA for specific projects implemented by multilateral organisations (multi-bi or non-core contributions). Although the percentage of total gross ODA allocated to and through the multilateral system has been declining over the last five years, the dollar value has been maintained and it is allocated in accordance with New Zealand's strategy, and with improved multi-year predictability.

Recommendations

3.1 As its economy recovers, New Zealand should set out a time-bound path for growing its aid programme towards meeting the 0.7% UN ODA to GNI commitment.

3.2 New Zealand should continue to concentrate its ODA in countries where it is a significant contributor, in line with its strong Pacific focus and commitment to providing quality assistance at scale; outside the Pacific, New Zealand should prioritise LDCs.

4 Managing New Zealand's development co-operation

Indicator: The member's approach to how it organises and manages its development co-operation is fit for purpose

Main findings

The re-integration of the development programme into the Ministry of Foreign Affairs and Trade in 2009 has prompted significant organisational change. The effective delivery of New Zealand's development co-operation has, on the whole, not been interrupted as a result of this organisational reform. However, there are risks with New Zealand's approach to organisation and management and some elements which require attention.

Following the re-integration, a business model "refresh" was initiated in late 2010 and resulting structural changes were implemented from May 2011. The structure of the International Development Group reflects the policy and geographic priorities of the development programme. The thematic and sectoral advisory function works across the divisions with the intention of bringing policy, advisory and programming together in a matrix approach. This would appear to be an appropriate structure for delivering on New Zealand's priorities and commitments.

The International Development Group's business practices have been re-vamped, as recommended in the last peer review. New and updated business processes for activity management were rolled out to staff from July 2011, with programme management business processes following in early 2012. There is improved and more streamlined design, appraisal and monitoring practice. Systems and capability to support a stronger focus on managing for development results have been enhanced. Management exercise strategic oversight on results, expenditure, human resources and on-going projects through, for example, the Leadership Team's "dashboard".

In line with its comparative advantage, New Zealand is able to leverage expertise in several areas of public policy, across government, to build capacity in the Pacific region. The ministry has entered into partnership arrangements with other key government agencies with an interest in Pacific (and broader) development outcomes.

The International Development Group has also shown a commitment to innovation, a core value of the Ministry of Foreign Affairs and Trade.

The International Development Group has reviewed the impact of organisational change and taken remedial measures as a result. There is, however, room for improvement. The ministry-wide "collective ambition" process offers the development programme an opportunity to further contribute to and influence New Zealand's overall foreign policy aims. The International Development Group is also continuing to look at other ways of harnessing the full potential of New Zealand's resources for international development through stronger whole-of-government approaches. The ministry's planned Pacific strategy, which will establish a regional framework for New Zealand's engagement with the region, should enable the International Development Group to influence and improve whole-of-government co-ordination.

Systems have not kept pace with broader organisational changes and management needs. As New Zealand has itself identified, and is addressing, the information management system is not fit for purpose, creating inefficiencies and duplication.

Design and decision making have not been further decentralised to country offices. As witnessed in Kiribati, however, designing country strategies, programmes and activities from country offices would enhance country ownership, responsiveness and flexibility, build on knowledge of local institutional constraints and risks, and draw on lessons from past experience.

To its credit, through the course of re-integration, the programme has retained a core complement of development specialists. However, they are fewer in number, there has been considerable turnover and the expertise available in certain disciplines is stretched. The forthcoming capability review gives the International Development Group an opportunity to reflect on and manage risks related to its human resources.

Recommendations

4.1 To draw on knowledge of local context, to remain responsive to partners, and to improve development results, New Zealand should devolve further authority for designing country strategies and activities to its country offices.

4.2 In reviewing its capabilities, New Zealand should assess and address any human resource related risks to the delivery of a high impact and cost effective development co-operation programme.

5 New Zealand's development co-operation delivery and partnerships

Indicator: The member's approach to how it delivers its programme leads to quality assistance in partner countries, maximising the impact of its support, as defined in Busan

Main findings

New Zealand is strongly committed to effective development co-operation, as demonstrated by staff and through the design and delivery of programmes and partnerships.

New Zealand now provides multi-year predictability across the programme, meeting the 2010 peer review recommendation. This includes multi-year commitments to priority multilateral partners, and four-year resource allocations for partner countries. The new country level Forward Aid Plans, systematically shared with partners, outline bilateral programming – both planned and underway – for at least three, and sometimes up to five, years. There is also the possibility to carry over funds, reducing the pressure to disburse, and the related risk of rushed and inappropriate programming decisions.

New Zealand's programming is closely aligned to national priorities in its partner countries. There are encouraging efforts to use country systems, including in difficult contexts, responding to the recommendation of the 2010 peer review. Providing budget support in Kiribati, in partnership with multilateral development banks, is designed to create strong incentives for economic reforms. This results-driven approach to conditionality could – once evaluated – provide useful lessons for other donors.

Development partners in the Pacific have committed to division of labour, and participation in country-led co-ordination mechanisms, through the Forum Compact. Regular meetings – regionally and in-country – help implement these commitments. Joint sector programmes are well embedded in the Pacific: New Zealand works closely with Australia, including through delegated co-operation arrangements.

There is a clear and demonstrated commitment – through the Forum Compact and through Joint Commitments between New Zealand and the partner country – to mutual accountability. In 2014 New Zealand became the first development partner to be reviewed under the Pacific Island Forum Compact's peer review mechanism.

The approach to multilateral partners is strategic, backed up by predictable and flexible tools, and there is a promising new approach for engaging with the private sector. Good use is also made of government (including local government) agencies in the Pacific.

While New Zealand does not have a separate methodology for fragile contexts, its standard pragmatic approach to partnerships and delivery is well placed to deliver realistic and appropriate results in these countries. A longer-term planning horizon (often planning is on an annual basis) would be useful.

Three issues remain where New Zealand could build on its own good practice. Firstly, there is not yet a clear line of sight between different planning instruments. In addition, these planning tools are not yet whole-of-government, exposing New Zealand to the risk that individual efforts are not all aligned with national strategies or based on a shared view of the context.

Secondly, New Zealand recognises that it will likely need to support its Pacific partners for many years to come, and that building capacity will be a key factor in the sustainability of these efforts. However, despite some transfer of knowledge and skills through technical assistance, New Zealand has not yet reflected on how to support capacity building over the long term in low-capacity Pacific environments.

Thirdly, the Partnerships Fund, an interesting experiment to create a single funding tool for a very diverse range of partners, does not seem to be providing the right incentives to promote sustained engagement in the Pacific, nor to be attracting partners in a strategic, effective way. In addition, there is scope to improve overall engagement with civil society organisations (CSOs) to reach New Zealand's development goals.

Recommendations

5.1 To co-ordinate and align its overall development efforts in each partner country, New Zealand should use the country strategy process to clarify how its different planning instruments fit together, and ensure that these tools capture all programmes across government.

5.2 To enhance the sustainability of its programme in the Pacific, New Zealand should include, as part of each country strategy, clear steps on how to support long-term capacity building.

5.3 To maximise the impact of its support to partner countries, New Zealand should review the Partnerships Fund against the commitments made in Busan to inclusive development partnerships, and to CSOs.

6 Results and accountability of New Zealand's development co-operation

Indicator: The member plans and manages for results, learning, transparency and accountability

Main findings

New Zealand has developed a strong performance system for its development co-operation that enables it to plan and manage for results, learning, transparency and communications at all levels. This section takes each of these facets of effective performance in turn.

New Zealand has made results integral to its new operating model, structure and business processes. The International Development Group has made a concerted effort to build a results culture across the organisation. New Zealand's results-based management system appears to deliver simple, timely and useful information for both strategic oversight and activity management. At the strategic level, New Zealand is working towards using results data as soon as possible in internal processes, to maintain and build the profile of results data and their value to the organisation. New Zealand commits to drawing on partner countries' own data and systems.

However, like other members, New Zealand continues to face some challenges. New Zealand should take care not to create, through its results system, incentives for an exclusive focus on short-term output results at the expense of longer-term impact, change and capacity building. Country-level results frameworks are not routinely agreed as part of the Joint Commitments for Development process. There is also a tension between headline and activity-level results approaches.

Evaluation is well reflected across the different levels of New Zealand's overall performance framework. The new evaluation policy explicitly aligns with the DAC criteria for evaluation and sets out criteria and responsibilities for strategic, programme and activity evaluations. Under the policy, New Zealand aims to complement activity evaluations with more programme and strategic evaluations, and more partnerships in evaluation.

The International Development Group is making positive efforts towards enhancing the usefulness of evaluation for institutional learning and future activity. Firstly, management publicly responds to all evaluations. Secondly, a management action report monitors the progress being made in implementing responses to an evaluation's key findings, conclusions and recommendations. Finally, New Zealand also conducts syntheses of learning from activity evaluations and monitoring reports.

There is a risk, however, that the selection of evaluation topics, and the credibility of the findings, could be compromised by the evaluation unit sitting within the line organisation. There was also incomplete understanding in the Kiribati country office context of how to implement the policy through the planning, resourcing and use of evaluation.

The International Development Group has strong statements of intent on knowledge management. However, institutional learning could be improved with more effective mechanisms for sharing and greater use of evidence and good practice, particularly outside Wellington.

The ministry's aid management information technology system is limiting progress on transparency commitments, despite some progress at the activity level. This system is in the process of being upgraded.

New Zealand has a good basis for communicating development results. It has developed a strong vision and narrative for its aid programme, and particularly its focus on the Pacific region. The results and evaluation systems are also now well placed to provide evidence and learning that can be used to communicate to the public and to partners. Taken together, these factors should enable New Zealand to communicate a very strong message about its development co-operation programme. These are opportunities, however, currently being largely overlooked by the ministry. Resources are not adequately directed towards a communications and development awareness effort.

Recommendations

6.1 To ensure results are central to mutual accountability, New Zealand should agree country results frameworks with partner countries at the same time as it enters into Joint Commitments for Development.

6.2 New Zealand should ensure the impartiality of evaluations is not compromised by the institutional location of the evaluation function.

6.3 New Zealand should continue to put in place systems and practices to meet its transparency commitments.

6.4 New Zealand should step up the priority given to communicating and raising awareness amongst its public of the development programme, through an adequately resourced and evidence based strategy.

7 New Zealand's humanitarian assistance

Indicator: The member contributes to minimising impact of shocks and crises; and saves lives, alleviates suffering and maintains human dignity in crisis and disaster settings

Main findings

New Zealand's experience as a disaster-prone Pacific nation has translated into an effective approach to reducing and responding to disaster risks in the Pacific, using its domestic experience and closely linking disaster recovery to existing bilateral programmes. Other donors could learn from New Zealand's successes in this area.

The new humanitarian and disaster risk reduction policy outlines a Pacific focus for the humanitarian programme, building on New Zealand's comparative advantage, and committing to build resilience, and respond to disasters in the Pacific region. The finalisation of this policy meets the recommendation of the 2010 peer review.

New Zealand has effective cross-government mechanisms to ensure rapid and appropriate disaster response in the Pacific, including long-standing co-ordination arrangements with the other major donors in the region. Collaboration on disaster response across government, under the ministry's leadership, builds on lessons from working together in domestic crises, most recently the 2011 Christchurch earthquake. Other donors could learn from this system.

A range of national, regional and multilateral systems provide early warning of impending disasters in the Pacific, which can be used to support early funding decisions. Bilateral development funding can also be repositioned for recovery programming when disasters strike. This helps provide additional funding for urgent disaster response, and also ensures that the recovery phase builds on New Zealand's in-depth knowledge of disaster-prone Pacific countries.

New Zealand conducts systematic after-action debriefs of disaster responses, supplemented by a consolidated lessons learned exercise at the end of each Pacific cyclone season; the results of these reviews are translated into learning for future operations.

Complex emergencies are largely funded through multi-annual un-earmarked contributions to the multilateral system, providing these agencies with both predictability and flexibility, which is universally appreciated. Larger scale complex emergencies are also funded by grants to ICRC or UN agency appeals on a case-by-case basis.

The Ministry's Annual Report on performance against strategic priorities includes some results information. Other reports made public are anecdotal in nature and provide little information on impact or results.

Despite the Pacific focus of the programme, funding may also be allocated elsewhere, as New Zealand seeks to play its part in addressing situations of grave human need.

New Zealand's criteria for funding decisions are very broad; this risks creating misperceptions about the objective and principled nature of funding allocations.

New Zealand's partnership with non-governmental organisations (NGOs) includes funding for humanitarian action by the Council for International Development, participation in New Zealand's Emergency Task Force, engagement on humanitarian policy and best practice, and funding through competitive funding rounds for pre-positioned NGO relief supplies and during Pacific and major global natural disasters. NGOs raised questions about whether the current funding modalities are as efficient and effective as they could be in addressing emergencies outside the Pacific.

The day-to-day workload is high for New Zealand's humanitarian staff. There is limited delegation of authority. Much time is taken up preparing briefing notes to inform decision-making. The largely operational response model supporting bilateral response teams across the Pacific is clearly an effective way for New Zealand to respond to disasters, and so this workload driver will continue. However, delegating more authority for funding decisions could help free up staff time for more policy reflection, and enable New Zealand to share some of its good practice with other donors and partners, especially in the lead-up to the World Humanitarian Summit in 2016.

Recommendations

7.1 New Zealand should actively share its good practices in reducing and responding to disaster risks in the Pacific with other donors.

7.2 To enable more efficient management of its humanitarian portfolio, New Zealand should review delegations for humanitarian responses, based on tighter allocation criteria that mirror New Zealand's humanitarian and disaster risk reduction policy.

7.3 To support effective partnerships, New Zealand should review how it engages with NGOs in humanitarian assistance.

Secretariat's report

Chapter 1: Towards a comprehensive New Zealand development effort

Global development issues

New Zealand has a reputation for being a good global citizen. This is partly related to its development friendly approach, for example in trade and climate negotiations. New Zealand has used this standing to advance the interests, in particular, of its Pacific neighbours and small island developing countries. Its membership of the United Nations Security Council offers New Zealand further opportunity to apply its "Pacific focus, global reach" outlook at a strategic level.

New Zealand has a reputation as an influential, fair-minded, global citizen

New Zealand is proud of, and seeks to reinforce, its reputation as a fair-minded, influential and responsive "global citizen" (MFAT, 2014a, 2012a). New Zealand attributes its membership of the United Nations Security Council in 2015-16 to this reputation,[1] allowing it to show leadership on its key strategic issues on a global stage. For example, it intends to use its Security Council membership to advance important issues related to conflict prevention, peacekeeping and environmental security, including ocean management, as it has already done in the negotiations on the post-2015 Sustainable Development Goals.

New Zealand has a strong record of advocating for and promoting global public policies that support development. For example, it is a long-standing advocate for trade liberalisation and a rules-based multilateral trading system through the World Trade Organisation. As chair of the agriculture negotiations, New Zealand has engaged in efforts to deliver outcomes that will support the Doha Development Agenda (MFAT, 2014b).

Similarly, New Zealand's negotiations within the UN Framework Convention on Climate Change (UNFCCC) aim for a rules-based global agreement that is dynamic and flexible enough to cover diverse national circumstances, and changing economic and environmental realities. It has also been advocating for the principles of effective aid to be applied to improve the quality of climate finance at negotiations on the UNFCCC (MFAT, 2014b).

New Zealand advances the global public goods agenda in its region

The government's "Pacific focus, global reach" framework clarifies New Zealand's distinct roles in the Pacific and beyond (MFAT, 2014c). New Zealand considers itself to be in, of and with the Pacific; it has close historical, cultural and people-to-people links with Pacific Island countries. It considers itself to be interlinked with the Pacific region in a virtual economy. New Zealand therefore recognises the importance of a prosperous and safe Pacific for its own prosperity and security. Beyond the Pacific, New Zealand is a niche development partner seeking to achieve impacts in selective areas where it has a comparative advantage. This includes transferring its experience of working in the Pacific to island countries in other regions (Chapter 2).

New Zealand is using its position in the Pacific strategically to advance the interests of small island developing states (SIDS) in international fora, as demonstrated for example by the recent discussions on development finance at the OECD Development Assistance Committee.[2] As a supporter of small islands, New Zealand has advocated in its own region and internationally for the right of states to protect and sustainably manage their ocean resources, in particular their fisheries. It has also been a strong advocate for eliminating subsidies that contribute to overcapacity, overfishing, and illegal, unregulated and unreported fishing (MFAT, 2014b, 2012b).

Policy coherence for development

Indicator: Domestic policies support or do not harm developing countries

New Zealand has the analysis, the policy commitment and the co-ordination mechanisms needed for a policy coherence for development (PCD) approach. It has positive experiences with using official development assistance (ODA) to complement domestic and foreign policies to ensure added development benefit. However, in order to make policies coherent with development aspirations, more systematically, new approaches to influence, monitor and co-ordinate will be needed.

New Zealand is committed to policy coherence, but over short time horizons and without measures of success

The *International Development Policy Statement* commits New Zealand to ensuring policy coherence in areas such as trade, migration, investment and the environment, with international development commitments and goals (MFAT, 2011).

New Zealand seeks to align and achieve consistency of development assistance and foreign and trade policy. This is the narrative that New Zealand uses in its policy documents, for example:

- "As a small donor committed to effective development, the New Zealand Aid Programme will build on our comparative advantage and align with New Zealand's approach to foreign and trade policy" (MFAT, 2011).
- "New Zealand's development engagement in the Pacific is seen as an important indicator of our foreign policy influence" (MFAT, 2014f).

In October 2013, the Ministry of Foreign Affairs and Trade commissioned research to identify and describe substantive opportunities to improve New Zealand's PCD (MFAT, 2014d).[3] While not accepting all of the recommendations from this research, the ministry used the findings to develop the *July 2014 Policy Statement and Action Plan on Policy Coherence for Development* (MFAT, 2014e). This explains what policy coherence is, describes New Zealand's position, provides some examples of action that New Zealand has taken, and outlines how New Zealand co-ordinates across government. This is a strong and explicit level of commitment to PCD.

The action plan includes a focus on inter-agency policy dialogue and establishes a prioritised PCD agenda, including identifying and promoting emerging opportunities in the Pacific through PACER Plus (MFAT, 2014e).[4] However, as noted in the 2010 peer review, PCD opportunities require sustained focus and action over a long period (OECD, 2011). New Zealand's Action Plan is cast over one year and does not therefore create an agenda over the medium to long term.

The last peer review also recommended that New Zealand set and monitor inter-departmental targets, with agreed indicators, in priority areas of domestic and foreign policies to further promote development concerns (OECD, 2011). New Zealand's PCD action plan does not establish indicators of success. It is unclear, therefore, how policy coherence is to be monitored.

New Zealand has mechanisms to promote co-ordination and awareness

The commitment to policy coherence is underpinned by formal whole-of-government policy co-ordination mechanisms. These include the requirement for New Zealand government agencies to consult on cabinet papers, and the oversight of New Zealand's international engagement by parliament's Foreign Affairs, Defence and Trade Committee.

The ministry formalises selected individual agency contributions to development goals through "partnership arrangements". These focus on the longer term (five to ten years), strategic and policy alignment, and results aspects of the relationships (Chapter 4). Funding is also available to other agencies through the Partnerships Fund (Chapter 5).

The research on policy coherence concluded that most government agencies were "quite well attuned to" the actual or potential impacts of their policies on New Zealand's developing country partners. New Zealand's policy making process was also found to be "reasonably well aligned to the government's international development objectives" (MFAT, 2014e).

Developing new approaches for wider and more systematic policy coherence for development

New Zealand's "development beyond aid" agenda focuses on areas where New Zealand can contribute to opportunities for better development outcomes. In the 2014 Commitment to Development Index (CGD, 2014), for example, New Zealand scored highest of all countries in the trade component. It has the lowest agricultural trade barriers, with low agricultural subsidies and no tariffs on agricultural products.[5] Another example is New Zealand's work on lowering the cost of remittances.

The Recognised Seasonal Employer (RSE) programme provides another example.[6] New Zealand has a need for short-term seasonal workers that is not being met by the local labour market. As a result, New Zealand has the largest temporary labour migration flows relative to its population in the OECD, equivalent to 3.6% of the workforce (OECD, 2014; OECD, 2015). The RSE policy provides an opportunity for people who may not qualify to live or work overseas under other immigration categories to earn an income, learn new skills and be exposed to new experiences in New Zealand. In the RSE scheme, Pacific workers go to New Zealand on temporary visas to work for accredited employers in the horticulture and viticulture industries. An ODA-funded training programme called Vakameasina is offered to 500 workers, including language training, budgeting and financial literacy, and asset-based community development.[7]

To further promote policy coherence for development, however, New Zealand will need to consider more widely and systematically the implications of its domestic and foreign policies on the Pacific. It is therefore encouraging that New Zealand is considering including a focus and performance measure on policy coherence in the next generation of partnership arrangements,[8] to complement whole-of-government support to the Pacific with greater focus on coherence between development and domestic policies. The ministry's "collective ambition" and Pacific strategy processes provide similar opportunities in relation to foreign and trade policies (Chapter 4).

Financing for development

Indicator: The member engages in development finance in addition to ODA

Besides remittances, ODA is by far the largest resource flow from New Zealand to developing countries. New Zealand is increasingly looking at using ODA to partner with the private sector and leverage private investments. This effort will require additional resources and programming flexibility.

New Zealand has developed an ambitious private sector strategy

New Zealand is developing a promising and strategic approach to working with the private sector based on lessons from past experience, and with a focus on leveraging New Zealand's comparative advantage, particularly in the energy, fisheries, agriculture, and tourism sectors. The approach is being built upon a strong understanding of the diversity in Pacific markets and the need to bring in relevant expertise (e.g. through expert panels). The Pacific Energy Summit is an example of how New Zealand is successfully using ODA as a catalyst for private investments for sustainable development (Box 1.1).

New Zealand will need to ensure suitable in-house expertise, adequate resources, and flexibility in applying programming tools to implement this vision, as well as a focus on tracking its development impact. It will also need to guard against merging commercial and development interests, which could result in increased tied aid.

In addition, New Zealand's Export Credit Office (NZECO) supports equity investments in viable infrastructure projects, including in developing countries, by offering to underwrite a large portion of the debt. Furthermore, NZECO underwrites New Zealand exporters' risk of non-payment by developing country government buyers, as well as risk of non-performance of a project in developing countries, where the funder/buyer requires performance bonds. If New Zealand companies request political risk insurance, NZECO refers to them to the Multilateral Investment Guarantee Agency of the World Bank. The New Zealand Treasury oversees the NZECO (Miyamoto and Biousse, 2014).

Box 1.1 The Pacific Energy Summit

In most Pacific countries, less than 10% of electricity comes from renewable sources. Across the region, around 80% of energy generation comes from diesel generation and 10% of the region's GDP goes towards importing fossil fuels. The economic and environmental benefits of shifting towards renewable sources are clear. The Pacific Energy Summit sought to turn "energy talk" into "energy action" with the goal of increasing access to renewable energy, and reducing the region's dependence on fossil fuels. The summit, co-hosted by New Zealand and the European Union in March 2013 in Auckland, brought together leaders from Pacific nations, regional and international organisations, private sector companies, and NGOs. Over 600 people attended.

Developing country partners provided a prospectus of investments that donors, through consortium partnerships, agreed to finance. New Zealand's NZD 80 million investments leveraged approximately NZD 635 million to fund more than 40 renewable energy initiatives across 13 countries. This includes NZD 255 million in grant funding and NZD 380 million in concessional loans. Investors included co-hosts New Zealand and the European Union; co-sponsors Australia, the Asian Development Bank (ADB), and the World Bank Group; and the European Investment Bank, the Japan International Co-operation Agency, and the United Arab Emirates. New Zealand sees potential for the Energy Summit to be used as a replicable model for other regions.

Source: MFAT (2014b, 2014c).

In 2015, New Zealand also became the first OECD country to join other prospective founding members in negotiations to establish the Asian Infrastructure Investment Bank.

New Zealand is not tracking non-ODA flows

The Ministry of Foreign Affairs and Trade formally tracks and reports ODA and other official flows to the OECD. The Council for International Development[9] tracks and reports aid provided by NGOs. However, the ministry does not currently track and report other non-ODA flows such as investment and commercial loans to developing countries.

As shown in Figure 1.1, in contrast to the trend in many Development Assistance Committee (DAC) member countries, ODA still represents a very high share of total resource flows from New Zealand to developing countries. Remittances, on the other hand, far exceed all resource flows reported in Figure 1.1, standing at USD 1.3 billion in 2012.

Figure 1.1 New Zealand's net resource flows to developing countries, 2003-13, 2012 prices

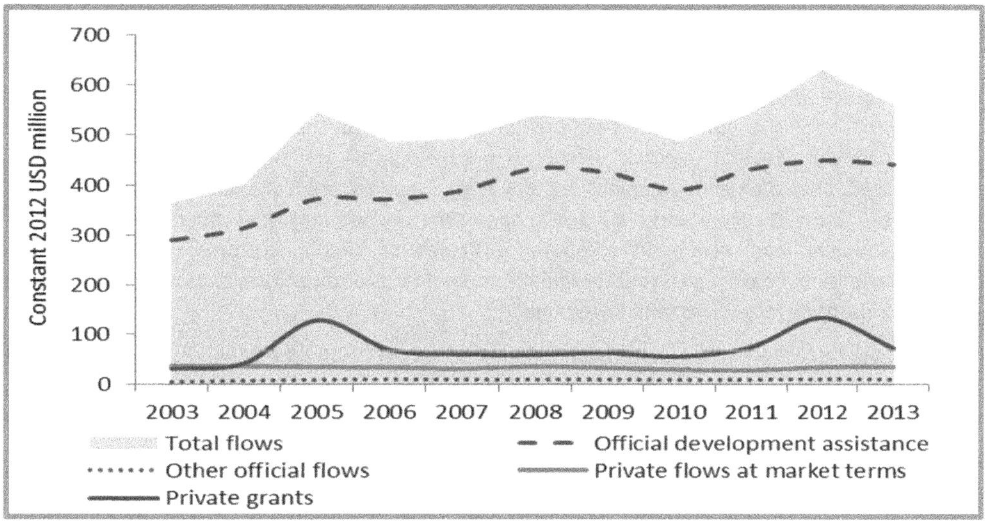

Constant 2012 USD million
700
600
500
400
300
200
100
0
2003 2004 2005 2006 2007 2008 2009 2010 2011 2012 2013
Total flows
Official development assistance
Other official flows
Private flows at market terms
Private grants

Source: DAC statistics.

Notes

1. See the New Zealand United Nations Security Council website: www.nzunsc.govt.nz.

2. The negotiated agreement contained several references to SIDS as countries most in need: www.oecd.org/dac/OECD DAC HLM Communique.pdf.

3. Specific areas for expanding the size and scope of policy coherence for development that were identified in the research included:
   - expanding the size and scope of labour mobility initiatives
   - safeguarding remittances to Pacific Island countries
   - shared procurement and procurement training
   - expanding New Zealand's pension portability programme
   - developing flexibility of risk underwriting for exports and services in Pacific Island countries.

4. "PACER Plus" (the Pacific Agreement on Closer Economic Relations) negotiations for a regional trade and economic integration agreement were launched by Pacific Islands Forum leaders at their 40th meeting in August 2009 (PIF, 2009). Underpinning this initiative was recognition by leaders of the importance of deepening regional trade and economic integration as a means to create jobs, enhance private sector growth, raise standards of living and advance the region's sustainable economic development. Several negotiating rounds, inter-sessional meetings and technical workshops have followed the launch of negotiations in 2009. Forum leaders and trade ministers have provided direction to negotiators at regular intervals. The scope of the negotiations now covers: regional labour mobility; development and economic co-operation; rules of origin; customs procedures; sanitary and phytosanitary measures; technical regulations, standards and conformity assessment procedures; trade in goods; trade in services; and investment.

5. Each year, the Commitment to Development Index ranks "wealthy governments on how well they are living up to their potential to help poor countries." The index scores seven policy areas that affect the well-being of others around the world: aid, trade, finance, migration, environment, security, and technology. See: www.cgdev.org/initiative/commitment-development-index/index.

6. RSE was developed with input across the public and private sector, including the Department of Labour (now part of the Ministry of Business, Innovation and Employment), the Ministry of Social Development, the New Zealand Aid Programme, Horticulture New Zealand, individual employers and businesses, and the New Zealand Council of Trade Unions. It was launched in 2007 with five Pacific countries taking part. The annual cap of the RSE scheme was set initially by the government at 5 000 but increased in 2009 to 8 000.people In response to the Forum Island Countries' call for enhanced labour mobility during PACER Plus negotiations, the cabinet has agreed to increase the RSE worker cap by 1 000 to a total of 9 000 workers commencing with the 2014/15 season.

7. Details available at www.aid.govt.nz/media-and-publications/development-stories/february-2012/vakameasina-training-extended-rse-employees.

8. Arrangements with New Zealand Police and the Ministry of Civil Defence and Emergency Management are the first to be renewed in 2015.

9. The Council for International Development (CID) is the national umbrella agency of international development organisations based in New Zealand. CID supports effective high quality aid and development programmes, with the vision of achieving a sustainable world free from poverty and injustice.

Bibliography

Government sources

MFAT (2014a), *Statement of Intent 2014-2018*, Ministry of Foreign Affairs and Trade, Wellington, www.mfat.govt.nz/Media-and-publications/Publications/Statement-of-Intent/index.php.

MFAT (2014b), *OECD Development Assistance Committee Peer Review: Memorandum of New Zealand, Ministry of Foreign Affairs and Trade, Wellington.*

MFAT (2014c), *Pacific Focus Global Reach 2013 Year in Review*, Ministry of Foreign Affairs and Trade, Wellington, www.aid.govt.nz/webfm_send/552.

MFAT (2014d), *Research Synopsis: Opportunities to Improve New Zealand's Policy Coherence for Development*, produced by Sapere for the Ministry of Foreign Affairs and Trade, Wellington, www.aid.govt.nz/webfm_send/676.

MFAT (2014e), *Enhancing the Development Impact of New Zealand Policies: A New Zealand Aid Programme Policy Statement and Action Plan*, Ministry of Foreign Affairs and Trade, Wellington, www.aid.govt.nz/webfm_send/675.

MFAT (2014f), *Annual Report 2013/14*, Ministry of Foreign Affairs and Trade, Wellington, http://mfat.govt.nz/Media-and-publications/Publications/Annual-report/index.php.

MFAT (2012a), *Development that Delivers: New Zealand Aid Programme Strategic Plan 2012-15*, Ministry of Foreign Affairs and Trade, Wellington, www.aid.govt.nz/webfm_send/448.

MFAT (2012b), *Partnerships for Progress: Development in the Pacific 2012*, Ministry of Foreign Affairs and Trade, Wellington, www.aid.govt.nz/webfm_send/299.

MFAT (2011), *International Development Policy Statement: Supporting Sustainable Development*, Ministry of Foreign Affairs and Trade, Wellington, www.aid.govt.nz/webfm_send/3.

Other sources

CGD (2014), "The Commitment to Development Index 2014" (dataset), Center for Global Development website, www.cgdev.org/initiative/commitment-development-index/index (accessed on 18 March 2015).

Miyamoto, K. and K. Biousse (2014), "Official Support for Private Sector Participation in Developing Country Infrastructure", *OECD Development Co-operation Working Papers*, No. 19, OECD Publishing, Paris, http://dx.doi.org/10.1787/5jz14cd40nf0-en.

OECD (forthcoming), *OECD Economic Surveys: New Zealand 2015*, OECD Publishing, Paris.

OECD (2014), *Recruiting Immigrant Workers: New Zealand 2014*, OECD Publishing, Paris, http://dx.doi.org/10.1787/9789264215658-en.

OECD (2011), *OECD Development Assistance Peer Reviews: New Zealand 2010*, OECD Publishing, Paris, http://dx.doi.org/10.1787/9789264112520-en.

PIF (2009), *Cairns Compact on Strengthening Development Coordination in the Pacific (Forum Compact),* agreement signed at the Pacific Islands Forum Leaders Meeting, Cairns, Fortieth Pacific Islands Forum, 4-7 August 2009, www.forumsec.org/resources/uploads/attachments/documents/Cairns%20Compact%202009.pdf.

Chapter 2: New Zealand's vision and policies for development co-operation

Policies, strategies and commitments

Indicator: A clear policy vision and solid strategies guide the programme

New Zealand has a clear purpose, policy vision and strategies that guide its development co-operation. Policies and strategies contain a strong commitment to the quality of co-operation.

New Zealand has clarified its strategic and policy settings

New Zealand has set out a clear vision for its aid programme. The programme is directed by a hierarchy of policies and strategies, and guided by a series of plans, frameworks and commitments.

The purpose of New Zealand's development co-operation is to "support sustainable development in developing countries, in order to reduce poverty and to contribute to a more secure, equitable and prosperous world" (MFAT, 2011).

As recommended in the last peer review (OECD, 2011), the *2011 International Development Policy Statement* (MFAT, 2011) clarified the new strategic orientations of the programme, while the *Strategic Plan 2012-2015* (MFAT, 2012a) established a medium-term outlook, including five strategic themes and ten focus sectors (Annex A).[1] The *New Zealand Aid Programme's Sector Priorities 2012-15* (MFAT, 2012b) set out in greater detail the rationale, in terms of New Zealand's comparative advantage, expected focal areas and expected outcomes for each of the ten sectors.

New Zealand commits to making its development co-operation more effective, reflecting commitments made in Paris, Accra and Busan[2] and participation in the Cairns Compact on Strengthening Development Coordination in the Pacific (PIF, 2009), in all its policy documents (Chapter 5).

Decision-making

Indicator: The rationale for allocating aid and other resources is clear and evidence-based

New Zealand's bilateral ODA is increasingly targeted towards sustainable economic development and the Pacific region. Focus and scale are also being achieved by having more larger and longer-term activities in its portfolio. New Zealand is a strategic multilateral donor, with evidence-based decision making on allocations and active engagement to drive improvements in the multilateral system, including in its own priority areas.

New Zealand is increasing its focus and scale for bilateral ODA

New Zealand's policies and strategies, since 2011, have consistently increased New Zealand's thematic focus on sustainable economic development and geographic focus on the Pacific region. In approving allocations for each programme, the Minister of Foreign Affairs takes account of the overall balance between Pacific and other regions, and the proportion of sector allocable ODA to be directed primarily to sustainable economic development (MFAT, 2014a). New Zealand forecasted approximately 60% of bilateral ODA to be disbursed to the Pacific region between 2012/13 and 2014/15. During the same period, New Zealand set a target of 40% of sector allocable aid to be allocated for sustainable economic development, a target it is likely to exceed (Chapter 3).

New Zealand's geographical focus is a response to the Pacific being the second most "off-track" region in achieving the Millennium Development Goals (MDGs) and one of the regions that is most vulnerable to climate change. New Zealand is currently showing a strong political commitment to the Pacific. Despite consisting mostly of countries which do not fall into the "least developed" category, the needs of the region are significant and New Zealand is well placed to provide appropriate and long-term support to it.

New Zealand is pursuing "bigger, fewer, deeper, longer" activities with a "five plus" (programming at least five years and over NZD 5 million). As a result, the number of activities funded was reduced by 33% in 2012 and there has been a steady shift towards activities of greater value and longer duration (MFAT, 2014a). This is bringing welcome focus and predictability to New Zealand's bilateral programme, and is also in line with its shift towards more programme-based approaches (Chapter 5).

Further concentration and focus in the medium term

New Zealand is aiming to further embed this thematic and geographic focus through its new *Strategic Plan 2015/16-2017/18* (MFAT, forthcoming). It will increasingly aim for focus and scale through identifying "a set of new targeted strategic investments that will offer maximum impact and value for money while also underpinning New Zealand's wider international policy goals" (MFAT, 2014b). New Zealand is also increasing its small islands focus, transferring its experience in the Pacific into the Caribbean, the Atlantic and Indian Ocean regions. This should allow for the strategic and consistent use of ODA funding.

At the same time, through its new Strategic Plan, New Zealand could reflect on whether there is a continuing need to set sector input targets. There is a risk with such targets that they detract from country programmes' ability to implement principles for effective development co-operation, such as ownership and alignment.

New Zealand's approach to multilateral ODA is strategic and evidence-based

The *Multilateral Agencies Programme Strategic and Results Framework 2012-2016* (MFAT, 2012c) sets out the rationale for New Zealand's strategic engagement with multilateral agencies, including outcomes sought and the rationale for funding, linking agency mandates to the New Zealand programme's focus. This has led to phasing out funding for some partners who are no longer aligned with New Zealand's priorities. There is a "comprehensive" relationship with nine agencies and a "targeted" relationship with eight, plus "niche" support for ten more agencies. The levels of engagement for each category are well defined in the Framework (MFAT, 2012c). For the 2012/13-2014/15 triennium, 78% of New Zealand's core multilateral funding has been allocated to organisations in the comprehensive category and 16% in the targeted. This layered approach to the multilateral system is both strategic and a good use of limited resources.

New Zealand applies the following criteria for making funding decisions, which are re-assessed annually:

- alignment with New Zealand's aid programme strategy
- alignment with New Zealand's foreign policy, including international development objectives, effectiveness and impact
- organisational performance
- international role and mandate of the organisation
- New Zealand's capacity to participate effectively in the intergovernmental governance process and other mechanisms for engagement between agencies and contributors (MFAT, 2012c).

In line with best practice, New Zealand draws on multilateral organisations' own accountability structures, complemented by other donor performance assessments, rather than conducting its own assessments. Feedback from interviews with multilateral organisations, carried out for this peer review, further suggests that New Zealand actively seeks to support improvements across the multilateral system and does not impose additional reporting requirements.

Feedback also suggests that New Zealand takes a focused and consistent approach, aligning its multilateral priorities with its own geographic and sectoral focus. In line with its Pacific focus, for example, New Zealand seeks to leverage multilateral resources for the benefit of the region and often acts as a broker for multilateral development banks in Pacific countries.[3] For example, during the successful conclusion of the International Development Association negotiations at the World Bank (the IDA 17 Replenishment Meeting) New Zealand helped secure a 33% increase in the "minimum country allocation" to NZD 7.5 million, benefiting many Pacific Island countries (World Bank, 2014).

Policy focus

Indicator: Fighting poverty, especially in LDCs and fragile states, is prioritised

New Zealand works in environments that are vulnerable, high risk, disaster prone and fragile, if not low income. New Zealand adapts its approaches to different country contexts. However, it is not clear how a policy commitment to poverty reduction translates into the design, monitoring and evaluation of programming. New Zealand has guidance for integrating cross-cutting issues, but limited expertise and declining resources to integrate them systematically across the programme.

New Zealand lacks guidance on reducing poverty

The Pacific focus is built on a long-term, deep understanding of individual country contexts and an appreciation of the diversity of Pacific partners. This includes an assessment of the multiple vulnerabilities facing those countries and peoples. Nonetheless, despite the policy commitments towards reducing poverty and vulnerabilities, there appears to be little guidance to ensure programmes are selected, designed, implemented, monitored and evaluated with a poverty focus. In Kiribati, for example, the review team identified missed opportunities to bring a more targeted poverty focus – in housing programmes, for example. It will therefore be important for New Zealand to be able to demonstrate, and not assume, that its increasing focus on the drivers and enablers of economic growth (MFAT, 2012b) translates into reduced poverty.

A pragmatic approach to working in fragile states

New Zealand does not seek out fragile contexts; however, it does occasionally work in these complex environments. Indeed, in 2012, 23% of New Zealand's gross ODA disbursements went to fragile states and contexts – including in Afghanistan, Timor Leste, Bougainville and Solomon Islands. Fragility is also a potential area of future focus for New Zealand on the United Nations Security Council.

There is no specialised policy for fragile states, but New Zealand has signed the New Deal for Engagement in Fragile States (IDPS, 2011). New Zealand's guidelines for applying aid effectiveness in fragile states draws on the New Deal principles, and provide a useful guide on how to apply them in practice (MFAT, 2008); this is appropriate.

Opportunities to support recovery and resilience are being picked up

The Pacific focus provides useful opportunities for New Zealand to support recovery from disasters (and thus link humanitarian and development programming), using its in-country knowledge and networks to tailor recovery programmes to the context. New Zealand also effectively uses its domestic experience to boost resilience to disasters and climate change in the Pacific and Southeast Asia.

Capacity constraints on cross-cutting issues

New Zealand has prioritised three cross-cutting issues to underpin its sectoral focus, to ensure good development outcomes, and to manage risks – environment, gender and human rights. There is a consistent emphasis on these cross-cutting issues in New Zealand's policy statement, strategic plan and sector priorities documents. The stated ambition is to effectively integrate cross-cutting issues into all policies, programmes and activities. A three-year strategy on cross cutting issues was approved in 2012 to build staff capability, to integrate these issues into business processes, to reinforce leadership and accountability, to manage specific activities and to strengthen policy advice (MFAT, 2012d).

There is limited evidence to suggest, however, that this strategy has improved the integration of cross-cutting issues into all aspects of New Zealand's development co-operation. As the review team saw in Kiribati, there is not a clear integration and monitoring of all cross-cutting issues in all programmes, and limited policy dialogue in these areas. Syntheses of activity evaluations also highlight the need for improved consideration and mainstreaming of cross-cutting issues in programming (MFAT, 2014c). This would appear to reflect, most significantly, a lack of capacity and sufficient resources to advance mainstreaming at both headquarters and in the field. New Zealand would benefit from drawing on other DAC members' experience of mainstreaming cross-cutting issues (OECD, 2014).

New Zealand has an appropriate and significant environmental focus

USD 144 million of bilateral environment-related ODA was provided in 2013. Thirty-nine per cent of New Zealand's bilateral aid had environment as a principal or significant objective and 8% supported climate change, compared with the respective DAC country averages of 23% and 16%. Both levels showed declines for New Zealand in 2012-13 compared to 2010-11.[4] As with other members, the spike in 2010-11 can be partially attributed to the climate change "fast start finance" period (Chapter 3). A number of environment-specific activities also ended in 2012.

Compared to its peers, New Zealand's ODA for the environment is significantly more focused on local environmental issues such as local pollution, clean water and sanitation, sustainable livelihoods (agriculture, forestry, fishing and tourism), and preparation and response to natural disasters. This is appropriate to New Zealand's overall geographic and sectoral focus. Over time, New Zealand has focused less on climate change mitigation than its peers. This may be linked to the more limited and lower priority of mitigation options in the Pacific, compared to, for example, adaptation to climate change or protection against invasive alien species, linked to biodiversity.

High but declining levels of support to gender equality; limited expertise

USD 130 million of bilateral ODA supported gender equality in 2013. In the same year, 50% of New Zealand's bilateral sector allocable aid had gender equality and women's empowerment as a principal or significant objective, compared with the DAC country average of 33%. This share, as well as the volume, has been decreasing since 2007-08. A high share of ODA to population, reproductive health, other social infrastructure and education focuses on gender, but less on the economic and productive sectors that New Zealand is currently prioritising.[5]

New Zealand has one gender equality advisor, with no delegated authority or budget. There are no staff with specific responsibility for gender equality in any of the country missions, as was evident in Kiribati. New Zealand therefore has very limited capacity to pursue a mainstreaming agenda on gender equality.

Notes

1. The five themes are:
   - improved economic well-being
   - improved human development outcomes
   - improved resilience and recovery from emergencies
   - improved governance, security and conditions for peace
   - improved development outcomes through strategic partnerships with others.

   The ten sectors are: agriculture, fisheries, tourism, renewable energy, transport and communication infrastructure, private sector development, education and training, health, water supply and sanitation, and safe and secure communities.

2. See: http://www.oecd.org/dac/effectiveness/ for more details on each of the three agreements.

3. "Proportion of multilateral funding directed to the Pacific (for high priority agencies)" is one of New Zealand's thirty headline results indicators in its Strategic Results Framework (Chapter 6).

4. Bilateral ODA in support of global and local environment objectives, two-year averages:

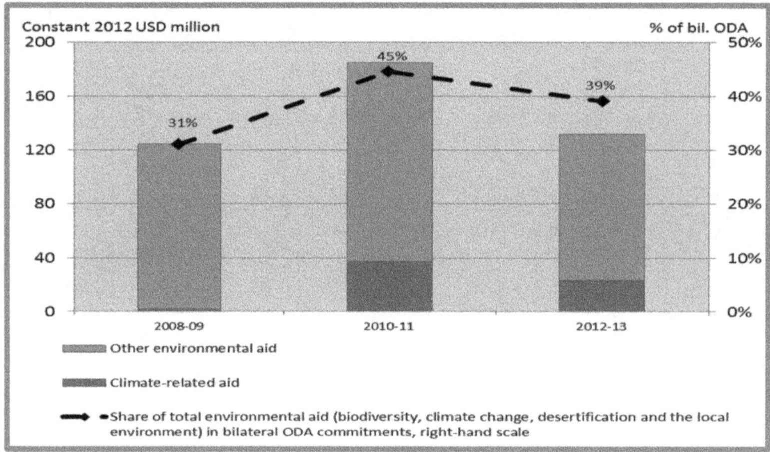

Source: DAC statistics.

5. Share of bilateral ODA in support of gender equality by sector, 2013:

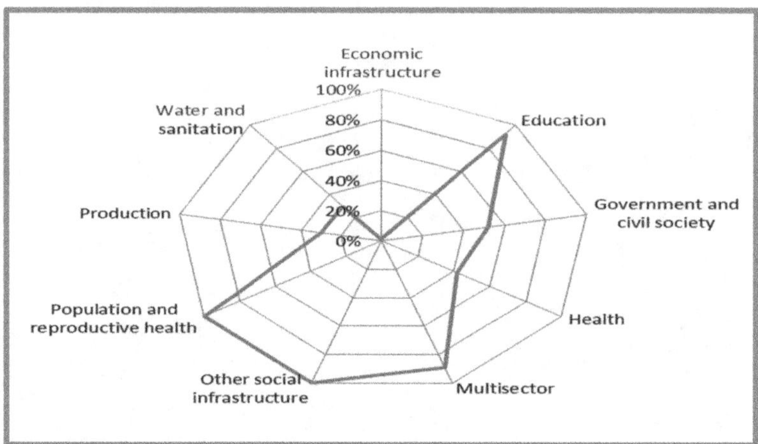

Source: DAC statistics.

Bibliography

Government sources

MFAT (forthcoming), *Strategic Plan 2015/16-2017/18*, Ministry of Foreign Affairs and Trade, Wellington.

MFAT (2014a), *OECD Development Assistance Committee Peer Review: Memorandum of New Zealand, Ministry of Foreign Affairs and Trade, Wellington.*

MFAT (2014b), *Statement of Intent 2014-2018*, Ministry of Foreign Affairs and Trade, Wellington, www.mfat.govt.nz/Media-and-publications/Publications/Statement-of-Intent/index.php.

MFAT (2014c), *What Can We Learn from Activity Evaluations?* Ministry of Foreign Affairs and Trade, Wellington.

MFAT (2012a), *Development that Delivers: New Zealand Aid Programme Strategic Plan 2012-15*, Ministry of Foreign Affairs and Trade, Wellington, www.aid.govt.nz/webfm_send/448.

MFAT (2012b), *New Zealand Aid Programme Sector Priorities 2012-15*, Ministry of Foreign Affairs and Trade, Wellington, www.aid.govt.nz/webfm_send/509.

MFAT (2012c), *Multilateral Agencies Programme Strategic and Results Framework 2012-16*, Ministry of Foreign Affairs and Trade, Wellington.

MFAT (2012d), *Strengthening the Integration of Cross-Cutting Issues into the New Zealand Aid Programme 2012-2015*, Ministry of Foreign Affairs and Trade, Wellington.

MFAT (2011), *International Development Policy Statement: Supporting Sustainable Development*, Ministry of Foreign Affairs and Trade, Wellington, www.aid.govt.nz/webfm_send/3.

MFAT (2008), *NZAID Guidelines on Applying Aid Effectiveness Principles in Fragile States and Situations,* Ministry of Foreign Affairs and Trade, Wellington, www.alnap.org/resource/9743.

Other sources

IDPS (2011), *A New Deal for Engagement in Fragile States*, International Dialogue on Peacebuilding and Statebuilding, presented at the 4th High Level Forum on Aid Effectiveness, Busan, Korea, 30 November 2011, www.pbsbdialogue.org/documentupload/49151944.pdf.

OECD (2014), *Mainstreaming Cross-Cutting Issues: 7 Lessons from DAC Peer Reviews*, OECD Publishing, Paris, http://dx.doi.org/10.1787/9789264205147-en.

OECD (2010), *OECD Development Assistance Peer Reviews: New Zealand 2010*, OECD Publishing, Paris, http://dx.doi.org/10.1787/9789264112520-en.

PIF (2009), *Cairns Compact on Strengthening Development Coordination in the Pacific (Forum Compact),* agreement signed at the Pacific Islands Forum Leaders Meeting, Cairns, Fortieth Pacific Islands Forum, 4-7 August 2009, www.forumsec.org/resources/uploads/attachments/documents/Cairns%20Compact%202009.pdf.

World Bank (2014), *Additions to IDA Resources: Seventeenth Replenishment - IDA17: Maximizing Development Impact*, World Bank Group, Washington DC, http://documents.worldbank.org/curated/en/2014/03/19330911/additions-ida-resources-seventeenth-replenishment-ida17-maximizing-development-impact.

Chapter 3: Allocating New Zealand's official development assistance

Overall ODA volume

Indicator: The member makes every effort to meet ODA domestic and international targets

New Zealand's progress towards meeting domestic and international ODA targets was affected by the Christchurch earthquakes and financial crisis. With the economy recovering well, New Zealand now has an opportunity to set more ambitious projections for overall ODA volume in line with international commitments. With the focus on the Pacific region, New Zealand is, and should continue to, allocate ODA to countries most in need. New Zealand is providing a good level of predictability and transparency to partner countries thanks to its forward-looking spending plans.

New Zealand is not making progress towards the ODA to GNI target

New Zealand was not able to meet its planned increase in ODA between 2009/10 and 2014/15. This is because of the twin shocks of the Christchurch earthquakes (September, 2010 and February, 2011) and the global financial crisis. Given these shocks, New Zealand is to be commended for the increase it was able to make in the ODA budget between 2010 and 2012.

Between 2012 and 2013, however, ODA fell in real terms by 1.9%, from USD 449 million to USD 441 million. Provisional figures for 2014 indicate a slight reversal of this decline, up to USD 489 million in 2013 prices or USD 502 million in current prices. The percentage of ODA to gross national income (GNI) fell from 0.28% in 2012 to 0.26% in 2013 (Figure 3.1), and provisionally to 0.27% in 2014. This is well below the target of 0.7% of ODA to GNI that New Zealand has endorsed, and the average of DAC members, which stands at 0.39%. Since the 0.7% commitment was made, New Zealand's recorded share of ODA to GNI has not exceeded 0.3% (2008).

Figure 3.1 Net ODA: Trend in volume and as a share of GNI, 1998-2013, New Zealand

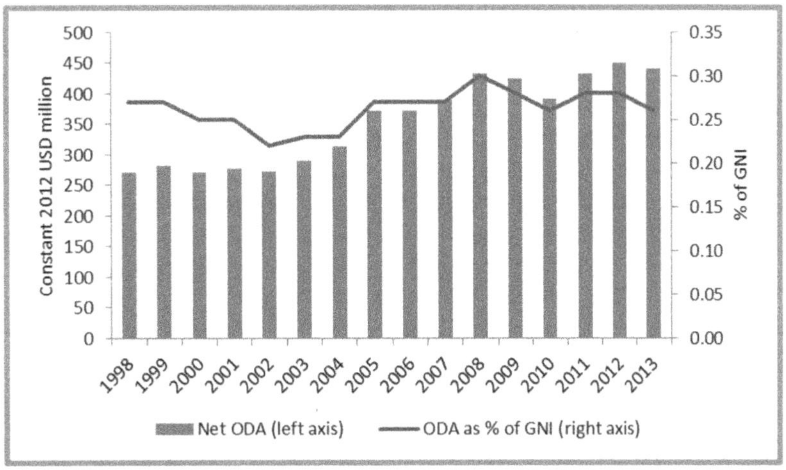

Source: DAC statistics.

New Zealand has set out its ODA budget projections for the next four years in its *Vote Official Development Assistance* (MFAT, 2014a).[1] The ODA budget is due to increase from NZD 589 million in 2014-15, to NZD 602 million in 2015-16, NZD 635 million in 2016-17 and NZD 650 million in 2017-18 (MFAT, 2014a). These projected increases are welcome. They are unlikely, however, to increase the country effort as measured by ODA as a share of GNI.

New Zealand's recovery from the financial crisis is progressing well (OECD, forthcoming). As New Zealand moves towards budget surplus, reviewing forward spending plans could also help it set out a path towards meeting its international commitment to total ODA/GNI, which will be especially important looking ahead to the 2015 events on development finance and global Sustainable Development Goals.

A small island focus impacts on least developed country allocations

In 2013, 32% of total ODA, or USD 148 million, was allocated to least developed countries (LDCs). This represented 0.09% of New Zealand's GNI, below the 0.15-0.20% UN target of aid to be allocated to LDCs and a little under the DAC average of 0.10%. As a share of total bilateral ODA, aid to LDCs represented 31% in 2013 and has been fluctuating around 30% in recent years.

New Zealand's allocations to LDCs has to be viewed in light of its focus on the Pacific region, which – while including many non-LDCs – also includes many countries internationally recognised as vulnerable and in need because of their status as small island developing states (SIDS).[2] Several of New Zealand's priority countries have graduated out of LDC status, and several more will over the coming years, including Kiribati – despite the immense challenges that country is facing (Annex C).[3]

New Zealand should, however, be careful to focus its non-Pacific, non-small island programme on LDCs in order for it to make stronger progress towards the LDC target. This would include its expanding programme, for example, in the Association of Southeast Asian Nations (ASEAN) region.

New Zealand complies with reporting requirements, including to partner countries

New Zealand complies overall with the DAC reporting guidelines. It reports its four-year indicative expenditure to the OECD forward spending survey (OECD, 2014). New Zealand's development assistance continues to be delivered exclusively in the form of grant aid.

The New Zealand Aid Programme consists of two three-year appropriations approved by parliament.[4] Its Strategic Plan provides indicative three-yearly allocations for each programme, including country programmes. Indicative information on future development expenditures is provided to priority country partners when programme strategic and results frameworks and Joint Commitments for Development are agreed. In addition, Forward Aid Plans are updated annually, so four-year indicative figures (i.e. current year plus three "outer years") are always available. Forward Aid Plans describe not just bilateral programme expenditure but also total country aid, including estimates of regional ODA delivered to that country and specific funding provided through other mechanisms (e.g. NGOs, other state sector organisations, and humanitarian and disaster preparedness programmes). This is encouraging.

Bilateral ODA allocations

Indicator: Aid is allocated according to the statement of intent and international commitments

Bilateral ODA allocations are consistent with New Zealand's strategic priorities. They remain focused on the Pacific region and increasingly concentrated among, and programmed within, priority countries. There are large increases in sectors related to New Zealand's focus on sustainable economic development, but education remains the largest sector. Governance support has declined.

New Zealand is consolidating its strong Pacific presence

In 2013, 77% of New Zealand's ODA was provided bilaterally. This is relatively high, compared to a DAC average of 73% in 2012, and has been consistently high (between 77-81%) over the last four years.

The priority that New Zealand gives to the Pacific (Chapter 2) is reflected in its bilateral allocations. Sixty per cent of bilateral ODA was forecast to be allocated to the Pacific between 2012/13 and 2014/15 (MFAT, 2014b). A total of 78% of bilateral allocable ODA was disbursed to "other Asia and Oceania" in 2012-2013 (Figure 3.2). This was the highest share of aid to Oceania of any DAC member, far exceeding Australia, the second highest, which provided on average 35% of its aid to Oceania between 2010 and 2012. Only 2% of total DAC bilateral allocable ODA was disbursed to Oceania in 2012.

New Zealand's non-Pacific programme has been reduced and consolidated in recent years. For example, the share of bilateral allocable ODA spent in sub-Saharan Africa reduced from 5% in 2009, 2010 and 2011, to 1% in 2013. In addition, bilateral programmes to Viet Nam, Laos, Cambodia and the Philippines have been consolidated, together with a new focus on Myanmar, into two programmes within the ASEAN region (MFAT, 2014b).

Figure 3.2 Share of bilateral ODA by region, 2012-13 average, gross disbursements, New Zealand

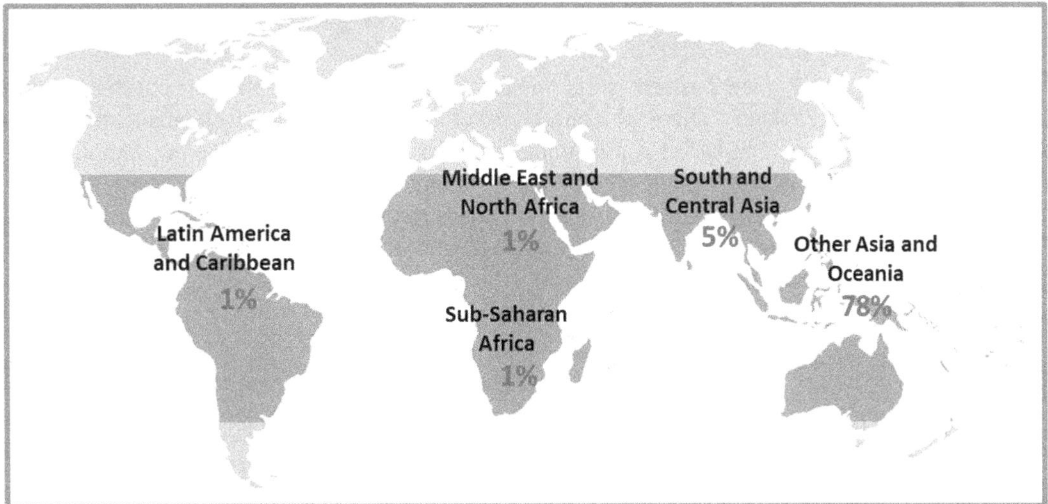

Note: 14% of bilateral ODA allocated was unspecified by region in 2012-13. This share is not represented on the map.

Source: DAC statistics.

New Zealand's ODA is increasingly concentrated on its focus countries

New Zealand has 15 priority partner countries, 12 in the Pacific and three in Asia,[5] all of which are among its top 20 ODA recipients. The number of priority countries has reduced from 17 at the time of the last peer review, due to the shift to regional programming in Southeast Asia. In nine of the 15 countries, New Zealand is among the top three donors (and the largest in three). In two of the 15 countries, New Zealand is not in the top 10 (Afghanistan and Indonesia).

Table 3.1 shows an increasing concentration of New Zealand's bilateral ODA among its top 5, 10, 15 and 20 recipients consistently over the last 10 years. In relation to the 2012-13 average, this is a slightly lower concentration compared to the DAC country average in the top 5 and 10 countries, but higher in the top 15 and 20 countries (Annex B). New Zealand is encouraged to continue to concentrate its ODA in countries where it is a significant contributor.

Table 3.1 Per cent share of bilateral ODA to top recipients over time

	2002-06 average (total 111 recipients)	2007-11 average (total 95 recipients)	2012-13 average (total 73 recipients)
Top 5 recipients	27	30	31
Top 10 recipients	42	47	48
Top 15 recipients	52	55	59
Top 20 recipients	58	60	64
All recipients	72	69	68
Unallocated	28	31	32

Source: DAC statistics.

A high share of bilateral ODA is country programmable

In 2013, New Zealand programmed 69% of bilateral ODA at partner country level. New Zealand's share of country programmable aid was well above the DAC country average (54.5%).[6] It is also notable that project-type interventions, although the largest share of New Zealand's country programmable aid, is well below the total DAC share of gross disbursement. New Zealand's share of budget support, on the other hand, was well above the total DAC share in 2012 and has been increasing since 2011 (Figure 3.3; Annex B).

Figure 3.3 Composition of bilateral ODA, 2013, gross disbursements, New Zealand

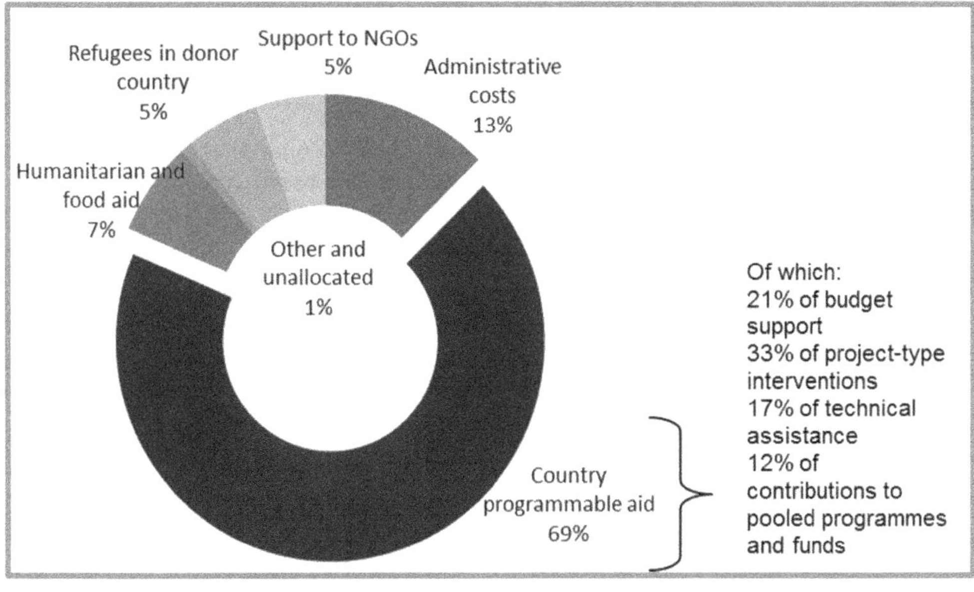

Source: DAC statistics.

Sustainable economic development spending is increasing; governance is declining

At the start of the current triennium, New Zealand set a target of 40% of sector specific aid to be offered in support of sustainable economic development. The target for human development was 36.7% of sector specific aid. These targets are likely to be met, and represent a doubling of allocations to sustainable economic development sectors compared to pre-2012 levels.

The sectors that New Zealand classes as having a sustainable economic development focus have seen the biggest increases over the last five years. These include transport and storage; energy; and agriculture, forestry and fishing sectors. Of the human development sectors, education remains the largest sector of support in New Zealand's programme, and health has seen modest increases (Annex B). The government and civil society and humanitarian aid sectors have seen a declining share of New Zealand's ODA (Annex B). As the support to economic development plateaus, New Zealand may wish to review whether it has a sufficient governance focus in its programme to underpin the achievements it is supporting in sustainable economic and social development.

New Zealand has met its "fast start" climate finance commitments

New Zealand made a three-year unconditional "fast start finance" commitment of up to NZD 30 million per annum for the 2010-2013 period, to support interventions related to climate change mitigation and adaptation in developing countries. It met this commitment, spending NZD 90.34 million to 30 June 2013, delivered primarily as grant-based bilateral assistance through the New Zealand aid programme. Fast start climate finance was used to increase water security, energy security and disaster resilience for communities and infrastructure. Fifty-three per cent of New Zealand's support was delivered to small islands and least-developed countries in the Pacific. Nearly 40% of New Zealand's fast start finance was delivered to support adaptation activities (Chapter 2).

Multilateral ODA channel

Indicator: The member uses the multilateral aid channel effectively

ODA channelled to and through the multilateral system is less than a quarter of total ODA. Multilateral aid is allocated in accordance with New Zealand's strategy, and with improved predictability. Core and non-core allocations are well-balanced.

New Zealand is a small but predictable contributor to the multilateral system

In 2013, New Zealand allocated 23% of total ODA as core contributions to multilateral organisations. It channelled a further 6% of its bilateral ODA for specific projects implemented by multilateral organisations (multi-bi or non-core contributions). Combined, this is a relatively low share of total gross ODA allocated to and through the multilateral system, and has been declining over the last five years (Figure 3.4).

New Zealand's total allocation to multilateral organisations is set by the New Zealand parliament every three years as an appropriation. New Zealand has improved its predictability by making multi-year commitments to its priority multilateral partners, as recommended by the last peer review (Annex A).

Figure 3.4 Share of ODA channelled to and through the multilateral system, two year averages, gross disbursements, New Zealand

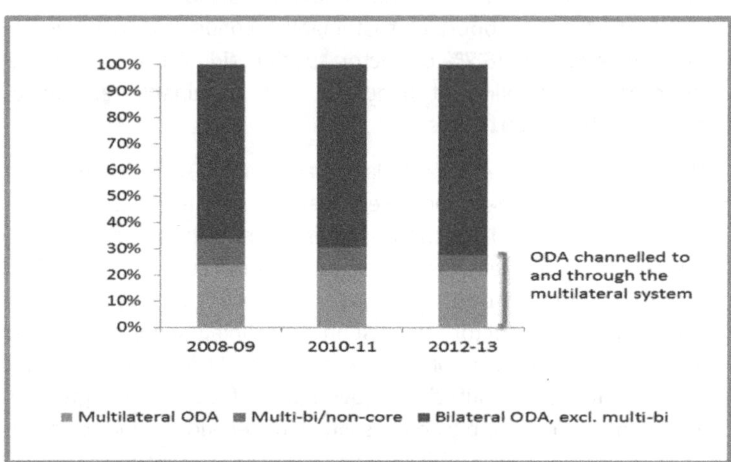

Source: DAC statistics.

Allocations are in line with priorities

A significant share of New Zealand's ODA goes to UN agencies: 10% of gross total ODA in both 2012 and 2013, compared to a DAC average of 5% in 2012 (Annex B). Contributions to regional development banks go entirely to the Asian Development Bank (ADB), given the presence of the ADB in New Zealand's regions of focus.

New Zealand provides non-core funding to specific multilateral organisations in response to prioritised humanitarian appeals, and bilaterally for activities which meet partner priorities and needs, relevant strategic priorities and New Zealand's quality requirements. Eighty-eight per cent of non-core funding was allocated to the Oceania and Far East regions, in line with New Zealand's geographic focus. The monitoring and quality assurance undertaken in support of New Zealand's engagement with core-funded partners is increasingly being applied in support of decision making on possible non-core funding.

Notes

1. New Zealand's development co-operation budget is primarily held in a separate "Vote for Official Development Assistance" (94% of reportable ODA). This vote is managed by the Ministry of Foreign Affairs and Trade (MFAT). The International Development Group within MFAT has primary responsibility for delivering the New Zealand Aid Programme.

2. See for example the exception for small island economies in eligibility for World Bank/IMF concessional loans. The exception states that "small islands (with less than 1.5 million people, significant vulnerability due to size and geography, and very limited credit-worthiness and financing options) have been granted exceptions in maintaining their eligibility" (World Bank, 2012).

3. Samoa graduated in 2014, Vanuatu will graduate in 2017, and Tuvalu and Kiribati are also expected to graduate soon after.

4. The New Zealand Aid Programme consists of two multi-year (three-year) appropriations approved by parliament: International Agency Funding and International Development Assistance. This three-year envelope is described in the International Development Group's Strategic Plan, the current version of which covers the period 2012/13 to 2014/15 (MFAT, 2012). Annually, the New Zealand budget ("Estimates" document) is presented to parliament in May and legislation is passed to reflect this. The multi-year appropriations are approved as separate legislation in the year of inception, but the expenditure within them is reforecast on an annual basis and published in the Estimates document. At the start of a multi-year appropriation the Minister of Foreign Affairs approves allocations for the three-year period based on indicative spend by programme and sector, estimated total country aid flows and the strategic focus and funding implications for each programme.

5. Fourteen of these priority countries are shared with Australia (of its 30) and three with Korea (OECD, 2014).

6. Country programmable aid is the proportion of ODA over which recipient countries have, or could have, a significant say. For more information see: www.oecd.org/dac/aid-architecture/countryprogrammableaidcpafrequentlyaskedquestions.htm.

Bibliography

Government sources

MFAT (2014a), *Vote Official Development Assistance*, Ministry of Foreign Affairs and Trade, Wellington, www.budget.govt.nz/budget/pdfs/estimates/v4/est14-v4-offdev.pdf.

MFAT (2014b), *OECD Development Assistance Committee Peer Review: Memorandum of New Zealand, Ministry of Foreign Affairs and Trade, Wellington.*

MFAT (2012), *Development that Delivers: New Zealand Aid Programme Strategic Plan 2012-15*, Ministry of Foreign Affairs and Trade, Wellington, www.aid.govt.nz/webfm_send/448.

Other sources

OECD (forthcoming), *OECD Economic Surveys: New Zealand 2015*, OECD Publishing, Paris.

OECD (2014), *2014 Global Outlook on Aid – Results of the 2014 DAC survey on Donors' Forward Spending Plans and Prospects for Improving Aid Predictability*, DCD/DAC(2014)53, OECD, Paris, www.oecd.org/dac/aid-architecture/GlobalOutlookAid-web.pdf.

World Bank (2012), "IDA borrowing countries", International Development Association, World Bank, www.worldbank.org/ida/borrowing-countries.html.

Chapter 4: Managing New Zealand's development co-operation

Institutional system

Indicator: The institutional structure is conducive to consistent, quality development co-operation

The re-integration of the International Development Group into the Ministry of Foreign Affairs and Trade has prompted significant organisational reform. The structure is now aligned to new priorities. Business processes have been streamlined. Integration within the ministry has also facilitated some improved whole-of-government working practices. However, there is room for improvement in the form of whole-of-government strategies in partner countries. Design and decision making have not been further decentralised to the field. Systems have not kept pace with broader organisational changes and management needs.

A period of significant organisation and management reform in the ministry and IDG

The last five years have seen a period of significant change for the organisation and management of New Zealand's development co-operation. Following the integration of the International Development Group (IDG) into the Ministry of Foreign Affairs and Trade in 2009, a business model "refresh" was initiated in late 2010 and resulting structural changes were implemented from May 2011 (MFAT, 2014). The changes sought to bring programming and policy together, and to support implementation of the new focus on sustainable economic development. These changes pre-empted, and in some respects provided inspiration for, a ministry-wide programme of organisational change that concluded in 2013/14, focused on modernising the ministry's structure, operating model and fiscal sustainability.

There has also been more focus on improving efficiency, and on speed and delivery, as part of the government-wide Better Public Services Programme. In the context of the development programme, this has led to an increased focus on partnerships, performance and results (MFAT, 2014) (Chapters 5 and 6).

Finally, at a more strategic level, the ministry has initiated a project internally to build a motivating and unifying "collective ambition". Staff engagement surveys had indicated that the ministry's senior leadership team needed to set a stronger strategic direction for the ministry and that the ministry needed more of a common purpose. A recent government performance improvement review also identified that the ministry needed a long-term strategic direction that better defined success. The project will define the ministry's common purpose as an organisation. It will set long-term collective goals that will direct, inspire and unify teams across the ministry to deliver. IDG is engaged with this project through representation on the senior leadership team and staff involvement in ministry-wide consultation. The collective ambition process offers the development programme an opportunity to further cement its position within and influence over New Zealand's overall foreign policy aims (Chapter 1).

New Zealand has good experience with whole-of-government approaches, but can do more at all levels

In line with its comparative advantage, New Zealand is able to leverage expertise in several areas of public policy, across government, to build capacity in the Pacific region. The ministry has entered into "partnership arrangements" with other key government agencies with an interest in Pacific (and broader) development outcomes. These include the Ministry of Primary Industries (responsible for agriculture, biosecurity, fisheries and forestry), New Zealand Police, New Zealand Customs Service, and Audit New Zealand. These practical partnerships enable the New Zealand aid programme to draw on the strengths of others and encourage a whole-of-government approach to key challenges and opportunities facing the region.

New Zealand is, however, continuing to look at other ways of harnessing the full potential of its resources for international development through stronger whole-of-government approaches. There appears to be a lack of reflection across partnerships in terms of capacity building and delivering whole-of-government support in line with development effectiveness principles. The ministry's planned Pacific strategy, which will establish a regional framework for New Zealand's engagement with the region, should provide an opportunity for IDG to influence and improve whole-of-government co-ordination.

Beyond the Pacific, the ministry is developing "New Zealand Inc." strategies. These strategies are plans of action for strengthening New Zealand's economic, political and security relationships with key international partners. They target countries and regions where New Zealand has existing or emerging relationships, and there is potential for significant growth. To date, IDG has only been actively involved in the ASEAN New Zealand Inc. strategy (MFAT and NZTE, 2013).[1] As more are developed, the strategies would benefit from being more integrated – making linkages between the thematic focus and aims of New Zealand's development co-operation, and the strategies and relationships being built around trade and investment, and security.

In partner countries, the ministry reports that heads of mission are exercising more oversight over, ownership of and engagement with the aid programme. The Forward Aid Plans also capture whole-of-government support in partner countries (Chapter 3). However, New Zealand lacks whole-of-government strategies at country level. Such strategies, building on the New Zealand Inc. model for example, would support heads of mission to exploit synergies between the different agencies, and improve overall coherence and co-ordination. This is especially important given that multiple New Zealand government agencies are operating in the Pacific at any one time – in countries like Kiribati, New Zealand's large component of non-bilateral ODA risks contributing to fragmentation (Annex C).

IDG has an appropriate matrix structure

IDG is one of eight groups within the ministry. It has five divisions: Pacific Development; Global Development; Partnerships, Humanitarian and Multilateral; Sustainable Economic Development; and, Development Strategy and Effectiveness (Annex D). The structure of IDG, therefore, reflects the policy and geographic priorities of the development programme. The thematic and sectoral advisory function is embedded across the divisions with the intention of bringing policy, advisory and programming together in a matrix approach (MFAT, 2014). This would appear to be an appropriate structure for delivering on New Zealand's priorities and commitments.

However, the re-integration of IDG into the ministry could be further embedded in country offices. For example, New Zealand could clarify reporting lines for staff and managers; particularly the direct accountability of IDG staff to heads of mission.

Designs and approvals are Wellington-led; there is an unclear separation of duties

The ministry, and IDG, reviewed levels of devolution to country offices in 2011/12. The stated goals of ministry-wide devolution included:

- ensuring that decisions are made in the right place
- giving decision making authority to managers who have proximity to the work, understanding and insights to make good decisions
- making the most of the talent at the ministry (Office of the Auditor General, 2014).

For IDG, no changes were made to financial and programming delegations. The Minister has delegated authority to approve up to NZD 25 million, the Chief Executive up to NZD 7 million, the Deputy Secretary International Development up to NZD 5 million, directors up to NZD 1.5 million, and deputy directors and heads of mission up to NZD 500 000.

Design and approval of country strategies and programmes is led from Wellington. The function of field offices is to implement, monitor and evaluate activities. As witnessed in Kiribati, however, designing country strategies, programmes and activities from country offices would enhance country ownership, responsiveness and flexibility, build on knowledge of local institutional constraints and risks, and draw on lessons from past experience. This was also the view of partner countries represented in the Forum Compact review team.

Further devolution of design authority and skills to country offices would also allow for a clearer separation of strategic policy, delivery and oversight functions. It would enable, for example, the centre to carry out quality assurance of field operations, including their alignment with New Zealand's policy settings.

Improvement of business practices and systems is a work in progress

IDG business practices have been re-vamped, as recommended by the last peer review (OECD, 2011; Annex A). New and updated business processes for activity management were rolled out to staff in IDG and to country offices from July 2011, with programme management business processes following in early 2012.

IDG has improved and streamlined design, appraisal and monitoring practice. Systems and capability to support a stronger focus on managing for development results have been enhanced (Chapter 6). Management exercise strategic oversight through, for example, the "DLT Dashboard" and its five key performance areas.[2]

However, this is a work in progress. As New Zealand has itself identified, and is addressing, the information management system is not fit for purpose. It is creating inefficiencies and duplication. Feedback from partners suggests business processes could also be further simplified.

Adaptation to change

Indicator: The system is able to reform and innovate to meet evolving needs

The International Development Group has adapted to the significant reforms of the last five years. It has sought to improve by reviewing these reforms and responding to findings. It has also shown a commitment to innovation, as a core value of the Ministry of Foreign Affairs and Trade.

New Zealand reviews the impact of change

A review of IDG's new operating model was undertaken in December 2011, seven months after its introduction. This review found that the new business processes were having a positive impact on quality and consistency. It made further recommendations for improving efficiency and effectiveness, many of which IDG acted upon (MFAT, 2014). This shows that IDG is committed to minimising the risks associated with organisational change. Further reflection on systems and capability is also anticipated, and will be needed, as part of the next strategic planning process.

New Zealand promotes innovation

Innovation is a core value of the ministry. The strategic plan identifies the need to be able to identify and better respond to ideas with the potential to help transform economies and people's livelihood opportunities, and to scale up those activities that have been shown to make a real difference (MFAT, 2012). There are strong examples of this focus being put into action, including in Kiribati.

Human resources

Indicator: The member manages its human resources effectively to respond to field imperatives

New Zealand has retained a core complement of development specialists. However, they are fewer in number, there has been considerable turnover and the expertise available in certain disciplines is stretched. The approach to staff development has become more systematic, but it needs to be applied to enhance skills in key corporate priorities. The forthcoming capability review gives IDG an opportunity to reflect on how to better manage its human resources.

Fewer staff and high turnover

Between 2009/10 and 2014/15, there was an 18% reduction in full-time equivalent staff available to the New Zealand aid programme. The total staff in country offices has remained flat over this period, including locally engaged staff (71% of all staff in country offices), so the reduction has been felt more keenly at headquarters (Table 4.1). A significant part of this reduction resulted from efficiencies achieved by integrating some services into the ministry. IDG is partially compensated by this reduction by being able to access staff time from the wider ministry.

In IDG, there has been a high turnover in staff, with 50% new or changed staff since 2010. This allowed for a significant recruitment in 2013, including specialist skills to match new policy priorities, despite the government policy to cap the size of the core government administration.[3] This turnover has, however, been felt by some partners in terms of continuity and institutional memory.

Table 4.1 Number of staff (full-time equivalent)

	2001/02	2005/06	2009/10	2014/15
Total staff in Wellington	79.00	105.50	186.00	140.00
Seconded staff in country offices	5.94	8.28	20.53	19.00
Locally engaged staff in country offices	17.48	27.58	45.97	47.00
Total staff in country offices	23.42	35.86	66.55	66.00
% Staff in country offices	22.87%	25.37%	26.36%	32.04%
TOTAL STAFF (FTEs)	**102.42**	**141.36**	**252.50**	**206.00**

Source: MFAT, 2014.

Specialist skills are spread thinly

The IDG is still comprised almost entirely of development specialists, with a small window open for exchanges with the wider ministry's diplomatic staff. New Zealand has retained, therefore, a core cadre of development professionals as recommended by the last peer review, in the context of re-integration (Annex A). Partner countries also welcomed the postings of high commissioners with a development background or expertise, such as those in Kiribati and Samoa.

Staff working in fragile contexts receive special compensation, such as rest and recuperation breaks, shorter postings and hardship allowances, to encourage them to deploy to these difficult environments.

However, it is not clear whether New Zealand yet has all the right skills in all the right places to deliver efficiently and effectively on its policy priorities. Specialist skills are available to assist the programme from Wellington; however, this appears to be insufficient to support ongoing analysis, dialogue and monitoring in key areas (e.g. economics and cross-cutting issues). The upcoming capability review provides an opportunity to determine critical gaps in staff capacity and expertise, at both headquarters and country offices. New Zealand can also consider innovative ways of complementing staff skills, such as the more widespread use of medium-term, external technical specialists that were operating in Kiribati.

Embedding corporate priorities through learning and development

New Zealand has introduced the 70:20:10 approach to staff development.[4] This has been well internalised by staff, but deeper and more accessible training is needed on corporate priorities such as development effectiveness. Not all staff have benefitted from the newly introduced learning packages.

Notes

1. New Zealand commits more than NZD 50 million in development assistance to ASEAN each year, in agriculture, renewable energy, disaster risk management, and knowledge and skills including English language training.

2. The dashboard assists with IDG corporate governance by summarising and analysing key operational data on topics like expenditure, results, human resources and ongoing projects.

3. Full information about capping of core government staff can be sourced at www.ssc.govt.nz/capping.

4. The 70:20:10 model for learning and development is a commonly used formula within the training profession to describe the optimal sources of learning by successful managers. It holds that individuals obtain 70% of their knowledge from job-related experiences, 20% from interactions with others, and 10% from formal educational events.

Bibliography

Government sources

MFAT (2014), *OECD Development Assistance Committee Peer Review: Memorandum of New Zealand, Ministry of Foreign Affairs and Trade, Wellington*.

MFAT and NZTE (2013), *New Zealand's ASEAN Partnership: One Pathway to Ten Nations*, Ministry of Foreign Affairs and Trade, Wellington, www.mfat.govt.nz/downloads/NZinc/NZ-Strategy-ASEAN-2013.pdf.

MFAT (2012), *Development that Delivers: New Zealand Aid Programme Strategic Plan 2012-15*, Ministry of Foreign Affairs and Trade, Wellington, www.aid.govt.nz/webfm_send/448.

Office of the Auditor General (2014), *Annual Report 2013/14*, Audit New Zealand, Wellington, http://mfat.govt.nz/Media-and-publications/Publications/Annual-report/17-Independent-Auditors-Report.php.

Other sources

OECD (2011), *OECD Development Assistance Peer Reviews: New Zealand 2010*, OECD Publishing, Paris, http://dx.doi.org/10.1787/9789264112520-en.

Chapter 5: New Zealand's development co-operation delivery and partnerships

Budgeting and programming processes

Indicator: These processes support quality aid as defined in Busan

New Zealand shows a strong commitment to the development effectiveness agenda agreed at Busan. Budgeting and programming have become more predictable by providing multi-year commitments for bilateral programmes, partner countries and multilateral partners. Budgets can also be carried over, reducing the negative incentives and pressure to disburse funds. Programming is well aligned to national priorities and harmonised with other donors. Risks are actively identified and managed at activity level. There are encouraging efforts to use countries' own systems, including in difficult contexts. The results-driven approach to conditionality could, once evaluated, provide some useful lessons for other donors. New Zealand could now build on these good practices by creating a clear line of sight between its planning instruments, ensuring that its new country strategies capture and co-ordinate whole-of-government efforts in each partner country, and by being more systematic about building capacity, especially in low-capacity Pacific contexts.

Multi-year predictability, budget flexibility, and carry-over provisions to reduce disbursement pressures

New Zealand has made its aid more predictable through multi-year commitments to its priority multilateral partners, and by providing four-year resource allocations to partner countries, meeting the recommendation of the 2010 peer review (OECD, 2011). The Forward Aid Plans, shared with partner governments, include an overview of planned bilateral funding across government, for at least the next three, and sometimes up to five, years. The figures in this plan are indicative, allowing for flexibility to move funding from one programme to another. There is also the option to carry over planned disbursements, sometimes beyond the three-year government budget cycle, thereby avoiding the disbursement pressure that many other donors face at the end of a budget window. Many multilateral partners also now receive three-year allocations.

Programming processes support alignment to national strategies, but are not yet whole-of-government

In Kiribati, New Zealand has a programme that is well aligned to Kiribati national priorities, demonstrating New Zealand's commitment to longer-term engagement, and recognising the challenges faced by a small Pacific nation with low capacity, few resources and severe climate risks (Annex C). This context-specific approach, aligned with the Kiribati national strategy and building on New Zealand's areas of comparative advantage, appears typical of New Zealand's approach to development programming in partner countries. New Zealand could now build on this good practice. First, the new country strategy process provides an opportunity to clarify the line of sight between the different planning instruments:

- *Joint Commitments for Development*, high-level agreements between partner countries' political leadership and New Zealand's Minister of Foreign Affairs, outlining development priorities and expected results
- *Forward Aid Plans*, containing indicative funding flows over three years,[1] including for projects that are currently in the design phase
- *Country strategies*, a new tool being developed to capture longer-term, strategic objectives for individual partner countries

- *Strategic Results Frameworks* for entire country strategies and programmes (Chapter 6).

In addition, to ensure that all of New Zealand's efforts in individual partner countries are aligned with national strategies, based on a shared view of the context and well-coordinated, the country strategies would benefit from being extended to capture the entire whole-of-government effort, based on the "New Zealand Inc." model (Chapter 4). Finally, the strategies should be required to demonstrate how cross-cutting issues will be integrated and monitored (Chapter 2).

Good efforts to use country systems, including in difficult contexts, but capacity building could be more systematic

The 2010 peer review recommended that New Zealand move towards a greater use of programme-based approaches and budget support. In response, there is now a policy commitment to use partner country's own systems where possible and appropriate (MFAT, 2013; MFAT, 2014a).[2] Indeed, New Zealand has made some good efforts to use country systems, including in difficult contexts.[3] Providing budget support in Kiribati, alongside the multilateral development banks, is a useful approach designed to incentivise and progress economic reforms; this complements New Zealand's more targeted approach to projects and is indicative of a welcome shift towards greater use of programme-based approaches. When deciding whether to use country systems, New Zealand makes use of the public financial management assessments of other donors, especially Australia, reducing the burden of multiple assessments on partners; this is good practice. In addition, most of New Zealand's aid is on budget, even when it is not using country systems.

New Zealand recognises that it will need to support its Pacific partners for many years to come, with both ODA and non-ODA support. It also recognises that building capacity in these countries will be key to their sustainable development and the most effective strategy to gradually reduce their dependence on aid.

Projects and programmes in Kiribati included some transfer of knowledge and skills, through technical assistance and other forms of support from across the New Zealand government. However, this did not represent a long-term strategy for building capacity in a low-capacity environment, to complement the short-term output results being delivered through the programme. This finding was echoed in a recent synthesis of activity evaluations: "Potential risks to sustainability of activities were raised in all evaluations. Repeated findings across activities were that they lacked sustainability plans or had insufficient strategic outlook. This suggests that more emphasis could be placed on sustainability of activities after the period of New Zealand Aid Programme support" (MFAT, 2014b).

Risks are well identified and managed at activity level, but less so at the strategic level

Risk is taken seriously at programme and project level, as well as in the choice of partners. IDG has an activity risk register, and a partner risk assessment template that applies to investments through civil society organisations (CSOs), multilateral agencies, regional institutions and the private sector. The programme appraisal process is stricter if the programme is assessed as high risk; risk levels are also appropriately a determining factor for evaluations.

The peer team was reassured that the focus on risk in activities does not hinder innovation; the push for results has instead provided incentives for staff to find new ways of working – care must be taken to ensure that this culture remains. However, risk identification and management does not yet appear to be a priority at strategic level – meaning that risks to the overall success of the aid programme are not systematically monitored by senior management, and thus that opportunities for early risk mitigation actions might be missed.

Related to risk management, New Zealand is committed to taking fraud seriously (MFAT, 2014a). However, since joining the Anti-Bribery Convention over 12 years ago, New Zealand has not prosecuted any cases of foreign bribery. As detection levels of foreign bribery are particularly low in New Zealand, the OECD recommended that the ministry continue to raise awareness among staff working on the aid programme of their obligation to report credible suspicions of foreign bribery to the Serious Fraud Office (OECD, 2013).

Aid remains largely untied

New Zealand is to be commended for the strict application of the DAC criteria on untying aid, and could serve as a model for other donors. In 2013/2014 New Zealand reported 85% of its aid as untied, in line with previous years, surpassing the average performance by DAC members of 76%.

A useful approach to conditionality, based on the delivery of jointly agreed results

New Zealand's approach to conditionality meets the requirements of commitments made in Accra (OECD, 2008). The conditions are based on shared priorities, often documented through the Joint Commitments; the conditions are made public through the ministry's website; they are harmonised, often with international financial institutions; and they are clearly linked to the delivery of development results. In Kiribati, we saw budget support, co-ordinated with the multilateral banks, and documented in the New Zealand – Kiribati Joint Commitment (MFAT, 2014c), where tranches would be released based on the delivery of economic reforms (Annex C). A similar payment-for-results model guides New Zealand's sector budget support in other Pacific countries, with tranches released once key sector priorities have been delivered. This is a useful model that may – once evaluated – provide lessons for other donors.

Partnerships

Indicator: The member makes appropriate use of co-ordination arrangements, promotes strategic partnerships to develop synergies, and enhances mutual accountability

New Zealand takes a pragmatic approach to co-ordination, division of labour, and joint programming, both on a regional level, and in-country. There is a clear and demonstrated commitment – through the Forum Compact and through Joint Commitments – to mutual accountability. New Zealand recognises the need, as a small donor, to work with partners, and there have been clear successes from engagement with local and central government, civil society and multilateral actors. The approach to multilateral partners is strategic, backed up by predictable and flexible tools, and there is a promising new approach for engagement with the private sector. However, the Partnerships Fund – an attempt to provide one tool to engage with a very diverse range of partners – does not seem to be providing the right incentives to promote sustained engagement in the Pacific, nor to be attracting partners in a strategic, effective way. In addition, overall engagement with civil society organisations to reach New Zealand's development goals is neither strategic nor effective.

A pragmatic approach to co-ordination, division of labour, and joint programming

New Zealand has committed to active division of labour, and participation in country-led co-ordination mechanisms, through the Forum Compact (PIF, 2009). A pragmatic approach is taken to co-ordination in the Pacific. Heptagon meetings of the main development partners at high level are held regularly,[4] and regional organisations and structures, such as the Pacific Islands Forum and the Pacific Region Infrastructure Facility, are also useful for division of labour discussions. Outside the Pacific, New Zealand focuses on niche areas, such as renewable energy in the Comoros,[5] rather than trying to work in areas already covered by other donors, thus supporting division of labour. There is a long history of joint sector approaches in the Pacific (MFAT, 2014a); and delegated co-operation – for example delegations from Australia in the Cook Islands, and to Australia in Nauru; New Zealand could look at how these arrangements have led to more effective programming. In Kiribati the peer team noted that New Zealand took part in an informal division of labour among the few development partners, supporting government priorities, while also seeking opportunities to work jointly with other partners, for example in the health sector and in the scholarships programme (Annex C).

Clear commitment to mutual accountability at regional and country levels

New Zealand is an active partner of the Forum Compact, reporting regularly on its efforts to make aid more effective. It is clearly committed to mutual accountability at the regional level; in 2014 New Zealand became the first development partner to be reviewed under the Forum's peer review mechanism. The Joint Commitments, signed at political level between New Zealand and each partner country, give these development partnerships a clear purpose, and are thus a useful tool to support mutual accountability at the country level.

Success from engaging with diverse partners, but lacking the right tools for the job

New Zealand recognises the importance, as a small donor, of working with partners; there have been clear successes from working strategically with a broad range of partners in areas where they can most add value.[6] The approach to selecting and engaging with multilateral agencies is strategic and pragmatic (Chapter 2). New Zealand also has a promising approach to working with the private sector based on lessons from past experience (Chapter 1). Good use is made of government (including local government) agencies to build capacities in the Pacific (Chapter 4). There is also some triangular co-operation, for example through a partnership with China to improve water quality in Rarotonga.[7]

New Zealand uses the Partnerships for International Development Fund (Partnerships Fund) for funding initiatives that are identified by its diverse range of partners[8]. This fund provides short-term funding on a competitive basis, aiming to promote joined-up responses between very different sets of partners, aligned to the geographic and sector targets of the aid programme. However, the fund does not appear to be providing the right incentives for sustained engagement of partners in the Pacific, despite the recognised need for long-term involvement. Nor is it clear whether the way this fund works helps attract partners in an efficient and effective way. The peer team heard a number of examples of this, including:

- The highest number of applications came from Tonga and Fiji followed by Samoa, Vanuatu and Solomon Islands. The cost of establishing new operations in other areas of the Pacific – where needs may be great but access is difficult – is too expensive for NGOs, who must match Partnerships Fund grants with funds from their own public fundraising efforts.
- There is limited interest from the private sector because the fund does not allow profits to be made with grant money (regardless of the development benefit).
- Applicants focus programme proposals on activities that are more likely to be approved by the Fund Board – meaning that there are a limited number of applications for key areas like disaster risk reduction, which has only received about 4% of total available funds.
- In Kiribati, there were fears that investments by one government agency (NIWA – the National Institute of Water and Atmospheric Research) in data on water quality would be lost, if the Partnerships Fund chose not to fund the second phase of the programme; the fund is not country specific, so investments can move from one country to another with each new funding round.

It is time for New Zealand to review the Partnerships Fund, and to assess whether it is suited to meeting its stated objectives.

Engagement with CSOs to reach New Zealand's development goals is not strategic or effective

The 2010 peer review recommended that New Zealand review how it engages with CSOs to ensure good synergies between the aid programme and these actors; this recommendation remains valid (Annex A). There is no separate strategy for engagement with CSOs, although there is regular communication with the umbrella body, the Council for International Development, which also receives some funding for organisational costs. Funding for most CSO programmes comes through the Partnerships Fund, which is not working effectively. Establishing strategic objectives for civil society organisation engagement, applying lessons from the experience of others, would create stronger, more balanced partnerships to reach New Zealand's development goals.

Fragile states

Indicator: Delivery modalities and partnerships help deliver quality

New Zealand's approach, partnerships and delivery modalities are well placed to deliver realistic and appropriate results in fragile contexts, although a longer-term planning horizon would be useful.

New Zealand 's pragmatic approach to development is well suited to fragile contexts

There are no special planning tools for fragility, with the exception of introductory guidance to conflict risk assessment (MFAT, 2008), which partners are expected to undertake. The lack of special tools is not a major problem – New Zealand's pragmatic overall approach to development is well suited to delivery in fragile contexts. However, a longer-term planning horizon would be useful in these complicated and rapidly evolving contexts – for example in Afghanistan there was a rolling one-year political mandate, which complicated longer-term planning, even though New Zealand understood that its engagement there would be for many years.

Active co-ordination with other development partners for coherence in fragile contexts

New Zealand actively co-ordinates and harmonises with other development partners in fragile contexts. The engagement in Afghanistan, alongside military support, was initially based on a whole-of-government effort to support the work of the United Nations. In the Solomon Islands, where New Zealand responded to a request to restore order and rebuild services after five years of conflict,[9] there has been strong harmonisation with other partners, especially Australia, and through the donor core economic working group,[10] in public financial management and economic governance. In Timor Leste, New Zealand has delegated co-operation agreements with Ireland and the United States, and has also supported pooled funding.

Tools and partnerships adapt to evolving contexts in each fragile state

In Afghanistan, delivery began – like many donors – through a Provincial Reconstruction Team and NGO partners, but since 2010 leadership of the programme has shifted to the Ministry of Foreign Affairs and Trade, which works in partnership with the provincial government in Bamyan. The programme's focus has also shifted, over time, from security to sustainable economic development, agriculture and renewable energy, reflecting the changing situation on the ground. A similar evolution has taken place in Timor Leste, and New Zealand's primary partnership there is now with the Timorese government. New Zealand can also use country systems in fragile contexts – as it did successfully in the Solomon Islands.

Notes

1. The Forward Aid Plans include bilateral funding, shares of regional funding allocations, scholarships and also funding from the Partnerships Fund.

2. "MFAT will uphold international commitments. New Zealand has committed to use country systems in support of activities managed by the public sector. Where the full use of country systems is not possible, New Zealand has committed to stating the reasons for non-use, and discussing with government what would be required to move towards fuller use" (MFAT, 2013). "We assess, strengthen and, where appropriate, use partner country systems for planning, implementation, financial management, monitoring and reporting" (MFAT, 2014b).

3. Most of New Zealand's programmes use country systems to some extent; New Zealand provides sector budget support to six Pacific countries, and general budget support to four Pacific countries (MFAT, 2014a).

4. The Heptagons are regular aid co-ordination meetings involving Australia, New Zealand, Japan, the European Union, the Asian Development Bank, the World Bank and the International Monetary Fund.

5. For more on this programme, a joint effort with the African Union, the Government of Comoros and UNDP, see: www.africa.undp.org/content/rba/en/home/presscenter/articles/2014/10/24/powering-up-households-with-geothermal-energy-in-comoros.

6. New Zealand's partners include United Nations agencies and funds, International Organisations, International Financial Institutions, Regional Organisations, other donors, Civil Society Organisations, State Service Organisations including Crown Research Institutes, local government, the private sector, and foundations.

7. More at: www.aid.govt.nz/media-and-publications/development-stories/september-2012/new-zealand-and-china-collaborate-world-fi.

8. Partners can also receive government funding by bidding for tenders.

9. The response was conducted under a mandate from the Pacific Island Forum, called the Regional Assistance Mission to the Solomon Islands (RAMSI).

10. This group includes Australia, New Zealand, the European Union, the Asian Development Bank and the World Bank.

Bibliography

Government sources

MFAT (2014a), *OECD Development Assistance Committee Peer Review: Memorandum of New Zealand, Ministry of Foreign Affairs and Trade, Wellington.*

MFAT (2014b), *What Can We Learn from Activity Evaluations?* Ministry of Foreign Affairs and Trade, Wellington.

MFAT (2014b), *New Zealand Aid Programme Making Development Effective: A New Zealand Aid Programme Policy Statement and Action Plan*, Ministry of Foreign Affairs and Trade, Wellington, www.aid.govt.nz/about-aid-programme/how-we-work/policies-and-priorities/making-development-effective.

MFAT (2014c), *New Zealand – Kiribati Joint Commitment for Development,* agreement signed in Tarawa in April 2014, Ministry of Foreign Affairs and Trade, Wellington, www.aid.govt.nz/sites/default/files/Kiribati%20JCfD%20April%202014.pdf.

MFAT (2013), *Use of Partner Government Public Financial Management Systems: Operational Policy*, Ministry of Foreign Affairs and Trade, Wellington.

MFAT (2008), *NZAID Conflict-Risk Assessment Guideline,* Ministry of Foreign Affairs and Trade, Wellington, www.aid.govt.nz/sites/default/files/Conflict%20Risk%20Assessment%20Guideline.pdf.

Other sources

OECD (2013), *Phase 3 Report on Implementing the OECD Anti-Bribery Convention in New Zealand*, OECD, Paris, www.oecd.org/daf/anti-bribery/Denmarkphase3reportEN.pdf.

OECD (2011, *OECD Development Assistance Peer Reviews: New Zealand 2010*, OECD Publishing, Paris, http://dx.doi.org/10.1787/9789264112520-en.

OECD (2008), *Accra Agenda for Action,* OECD Publishing, Paris, http://dx.doi.org/10.1787/9789264098107-en.

PIF (2009), *Cairns Compact on Strengthening Development Coordination in the Pacific (Forum Compact),* agreement signed at the Pacific Islands Forum Leaders Meeting, Cairns, Fortieth Pacific Islands Forum, 4-7 August 2009, www.forumsec.org/resources/uploads/attachments/documents/Cairns%20Compact%202009.pdf.

Chapter 6: Results management and accountability of New Zealand's development co-operation

Results-based management system

Indicator: A results-based management system is in place to assess performance on the basis of development priorities, objectives and systems of partner countries

New Zealand has integrated a strong focus on results in its new operating model, structure and business processes. It has made a concerted effort to build a results culture and to make use of results information across the organisation. New Zealand commits to drawing on partner countries' own data and systems and to support the development of these systems. However, like other members, New Zealand continues to face some challenges. Country-level results frameworks are not routinely agreed as part of Joint Commitments for Development. There is also a tension between headline and activity-level results approaches.

New Zealand's performance system establishes results as a central focus

New Zealand's aid programme performance system is used to:

- enhance management decision making in order to deliver effective and efficient development results
- underpin learning and continuous improvement
- provide accountability to parliament and taxpayers for the ministry's management of the New Zealand Aid Programme (MFAT, 2014a).

This system effectively creates a line of sight between policy, planning, monitoring and reporting (see Figure 6.1). At the heart of this system is a strong focus on evidence and results, at the strategic, programme and activity levels.

The Strategic Results Framework was established in 2012 as part of the New Zealand Aid Programme Strategic Plan (MFAT, 2012). There are three tiers for measurement and reporting:

- a set of high-level global development indicators, including the MDGs, not directly attributable to New Zealand's support
- a set of thirty headline, largely output, results indicators against New Zealand's five priority themes (Chapter 2), that are directly attributable to New Zealand's support[1]
- a set of operational and organisational performance indicators.

Although aggregate targets are not set against the indicators in the Strategic Results Framework, New Zealand measures and publicly reports on the percentage of indicators that are "on track", at both the global development and headline results levels of the Strategic Results Framework (MFAT, 2014b).[2]

In line with the objectives of the performance system, New Zealand has complemented the work on frameworks and indicators with a concerted effort to increase staff understanding of the importance of results management, including the importance of openly discussing negative alongside positive results. "Results leaders" and "results champions" are identified at all organisational levels to help advocate for results-based management (OECD, 2014a).

Figure 6.1 New Zealand Aid Programme Performance System

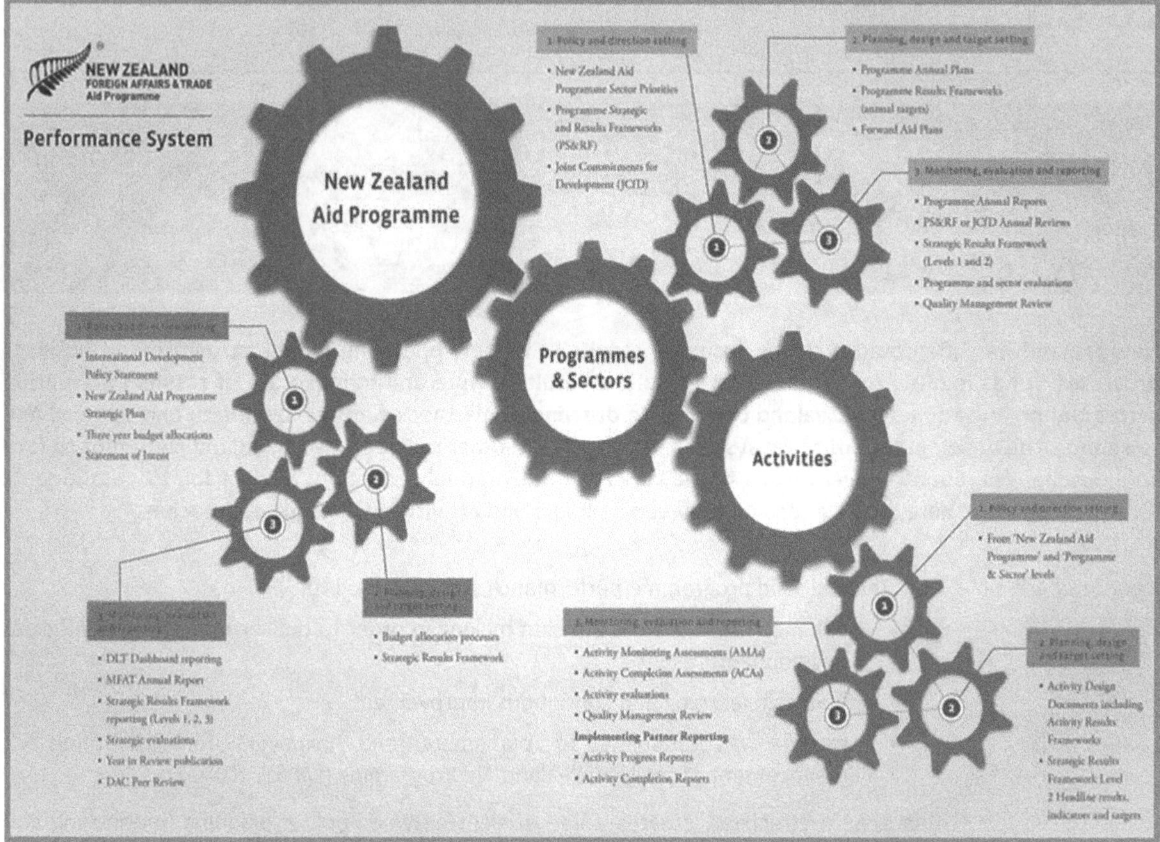

Source: MFAT (2014a), *Memorandum of New Zealand*, Ministry of Foreign Affairs and Trade, Wellington.

Results are used for management, and aligned to partner processes

The 2010 peer review recommended that New Zealand build on positive efforts for managing for results and knowledge sharing to develop a more strategic use of monitoring and evaluation for forward-looking management (OECD, 2011). New Zealand has acted on this recommendation as part of the construction of the performance system shown in Figure 6.1 (Annex A).

New Zealand emphasises the need to have specific budget lines for monitoring as well as evaluation tasks, such as data collection, in an activity budget. New Zealand's results-based management system appears to deliver simple, timely and useful information for both strategic oversight and activity management. At the strategic level, New Zealand is working towards using results data as soon as possible in internal processes, to maintain and build the profile of results data and their value to the organisation (OECD, 2014a). Staff have a responsibility for quality control before and after results are centrally analysed and made available for use. Annual monitoring assessments and completion assessments at activity level allow for corrective action in programming and lesson learning. The results frameworks for Joint Commitments for Development are also to be reviewed and revised annually.

New Zealand develops its programme-level results frameworks while being mindful of partner country results frameworks and approaches. It seeks, where possible, alignment between indicators, targets, and monitoring and reporting processes. Further, New Zealand's approach to the problem of unavailable or unreliable data is to strengthen partner country systems, and to partner with other organisations to share information on indicators. New Zealand has, for example, worked with the Australian Department for Foreign Affairs and Trade and with the Asian Development Bank (ADB) in the South Pacific to develop a set of standard common indicators to apply across programmes and activities. An internal database is updated every six months tracking progress against standard common indicators (OECD, 2014a).

New Zealand faces challenges as it continues to roll out the results approach

Despite the progressive approach being taken and the achievements to date, New Zealand recognises that the task of instituting results management is not yet complete.

It is unclear how the 30 headline indicators in the Strategic Results Framework are being deployed across the organisation. They are not referred to in the guidance for developing Joint Commitments for Development or programme results frameworks (MFAT, 2011 and 2012b). Accordingly, the most recent audit of IDG recommended that further work was required to align activity-level performance measures to the headline results indicators (Audit New Zealand, 2014). Yet, as mentioned above, the ministry has set targets for the percentage of indicators that are on track. This information is drawn from available country programme and activity headline results reporting. New Zealand could review and clarify the purpose of these indicators and whether they are impacting on New Zealand's stated priority of aligning with partner country result frameworks and data efforts. Similarly, New Zealand should take care not to create, through its results system, incentives for an exclusive focus on short-term output results at the expense of longer-term impact, change and capacity building.

In addition, the Kiribati country programme lacked an overarching strategic results framework against which performance could be measured. The guidance for developing a results framework for a Joint Commitment for Development (MFAT, 2011) does not require governments to sign Joint Commitments for Development together with a results framework. However, the Joint Commitment does identify the outcomes and results expected to be achieved through the Kiribati country programme. Failing to develop the results framework alongside the Joint Commitment would appear to be a missed opportunity; strategic objectives in a particular country could be linked with achieving development results, and results could be positioned as part of the overall mutual accountability mechanism (Chapter 5).

Ministry staff will also need continual sensitisation, guidance and capacity building opportunities in order to apply the results approach, and develop results frameworks, consistently across the programme.

A pragmatic approach to results in fragile contexts

In fragile contexts, New Zealand has a good understanding that it can take longer to achieve results than in more stable situations, and adapts its expectations accordingly. There has been a retrospective review of results in the Solomon Islands (MFAT, 2013a); this may provide useful learning for New Zealand's future work in fragile contexts.

Evaluation system

Indicator: The evaluation system is in line with the DAC evaluation principles

New Zealand's new evaluation policy aims to complement activity evaluations with more programme and strategic evaluations, and more partnerships in evaluation. However, the evaluation system as a whole is a work in progress. The evaluation process is not entirely impartial. There is also incomplete understanding in the field of how to implement the policy through the planning, resourcing and use of evaluation.

A promising new approach to evaluation

Evaluation is well reflected across the different levels of New Zealand's overall performance framework (Figure 6.1). The new evaluation policy (MFAT, 2014c) explicitly aligns with the DAC criteria for evaluation and sets out criteria and responsibilities for strategic, programme and activity evaluations.[3] The Evaluation and Research team, with three full-time equivalent staff members, takes overall responsibility for implementing the policy.

New Zealand has most experience with evaluation at the activity level. The last peer review recommended more strategic evaluations (OECD, 2011) and New Zealand now has a programme of strategic evaluations, some completed and some planned. Examples of completed strategic evaluations include the 2014 evaluation of donor support for tax reform in the Pacific (MFAT, 2014d; Box 6.1) and the 2013 evaluation of New Zealand's police support in developing countries (MFAT, 2013b).[4] It is also encouraging that New Zealand is planning for process evaluations on "how we work", such as one on development effectiveness in 2015/16.

Box 6.1 Evaluating donor support for tax reform in the Pacific

A well-functioning tax system is a critical part of any country's financial systems. It provides revenue for government to fund its services. In Pacific countries, taxation ensures greater self-sustainability and less reliance on aid flow.

The Ministry of Foreign Affairs and Trade commissioned a strategic evaluation of donor assistance for taxation reform in the Pacific from 2002 to 2012 (MFAT, 2014d). Conducted by the Sapere Research Group, the evaluation provides insights into the process of tax reform and how it might be improved to deliver better results. Reforms in 16 Pacific Island countries were studied. There were also detailed case studies of reforms in Kiribati, Samoa, Solomon Islands and Tonga.

The evaluation found that, despite improvements achieved in taxation systems, reform outcomes remain fragile. Reforms to date have focused on changing rules and administration infrastructure as opposed to behavioural change. According to the report, the fragility is partly due to donors' focus on short-term technically focused projects rather than systematic tax reform.

Significant improvements are predicted from donors moving to more systematic and co-ordinated engagement and dialogue with Pacific countries. This would entail donor countries working with these countries to focus on incremental changes to their whole tax system. In practice, this could mean supporting broad mentoring type engagements between donor country tax departments and their Pacific counterparts.

Findings from the evaluation will be used to inform and influence future policy and practice of donors, partners and stakeholders.

See: www.aid.govt.nz/sites/default/files/Synthesis Report -Lessons from donor effort to support taxation reform in the Pacific.pdf.

Impartiality is not guaranteed

The New Zealand Aid Programme's Evaluation and Research Board supports and enhances the quality and use of evaluation, and provides oversight and direction for the evaluation programme. However, it is the Development Leadership Team (Chapter 4) that ultimately decides what will be evaluated.[5] There is a risk that the selection of evaluation topics, and the credibility of the findings, could be compromised by the evaluation unit sitting within the line organisation. As the DAC principles note, "impartiality and independence will best be achieved by separating the evaluation function from the line management responsible for planning and managing development assistance" (OECD, 1991). Appropriate measures to safeguard the independence of the evaluation function could be considered.

Evaluations are planned and budgeted at the centre, but not always in country offices

A strategic evaluation and research programme (2013/14 - 2016/17) sets out a sequenced plan for thematic, programme and process evaluations, as well as policy research. The Evaluation and Research team has a dedicated three-year budget for the execution of this plan.

Activity evaluations are planned and budgeted as part of activity design or implementation. There are also Wellington-initiated activity evaluations involving country offices, for which the Evaluation and Research Team provide quality control. However, in Kiribati, there did not appear to be a clear plan, guided by the new evaluation policy and with input from the Evaluation and Research team, as to how and when to select evaluations. It was also not clear what role the Evaluation and Research team would play in the quality control of evaluation activity. This lack of planning and oversight may compromise the use and value of evaluations from both a programming and corporate perspective. It is encouraging therefore that the new policy is being rolled out with evaluation training to address some of these concerns.

New Zealand is developing evaluation partnerships

New Zealand has experience with both joint and partner-led evaluations.[6] The evaluation policy encourages partner-led or joint evaluations "where appropriate". Where partners lead the evaluation, New Zealand uses partners' evaluation systems and accesses the evidence they generate. It also works with partners, when required, to ensure DAC evaluation quality standards apply to promote evaluation quality, use and learning (MFAT, 2014c).

Institutional learning

Indicator: Evaluations and appropriate knowledge management systems are used as management tools

New Zealand learns from and demonstrates accountability towards evaluation findings. It also has strong statements of intent on knowledge sharing. However, institutional learning is hampered by the absence of knowledge networks that would allow all staff to access and benefit from research, evidence and good practice.

Evaluations are followed up

There is systematic and transparent dissemination of evaluation results and lessons. Management responds to all evaluations. A management action report monitors the progress being made in implementing responses to an evaluation's key findings, conclusions and recommendations, which is reviewed by the Evaluation and Research Board. New Zealand also conducts syntheses of learning from activity evaluations (MFAT, 2014e). These efforts are positive attempts to enhance the usefulness of evaluation for institutional learning and future activity.

New Zealand is missing knowledge brokers

New Zealand has developed a knowledge and results strategy with a five-year time frame (MFAT, 2013c). This has a strong focus on building an evidence-based culture. A programme of strategic research works collaboratively alongside the programme of strategic evaluations, under which one or two key pieces of strategic research are identified and commissioned annually.[7]

New Zealand communicates research, evidence and good practice through a programme of interactive sessions, seminars and workshops, which enable sharing of research, evaluation outcomes and other evidence as well as of experience and good practice on aid management challenges. A dedicated knowledge intranet site makes resources available to staff across the organisation, including knowledge notes and fact sheets.

Establishing knowledge networks and "communities of practice" could facilitate greater sharing and use of evidence and good practice (particularly outside Wellington). At the time of the last peer review, there were nine active communities of practice, which were reviewed as being useful in supporting and brokering knowledge management. Only one community of practice still functions. New Zealand could explore options for encouraging further sharing of knowledge to support its new knowledge strategy.

Communication, accountability and development awareness

Indicator: The member communicates development results transparently and honestly

New Zealand has a good basis for communicating development results transparently. However, resources are not adequately directed towards a communications and development awareness effort. Information technology systems are limiting progress on transparency commitments.

New Zealand is unlikely to meet transparency commitment

New Zealand has improved its transparency at the activity level. However, in the 2013/14 Annual Report, the ministry reports that only partial compliance with the Transparency Common Standard is likely by 2015 (MFAT, 2014b). New Zealand also dropped in the Publish What You Fund index, from 18th out of 67 donors in 2013 to 26th out of 68 in 2014 (Publish What You Fund, 2014). This reflects the constrained capability of the information technology (IT) system, in the form of the Aid Activity Management System. This system is in the process of being replaced, and New Zealand will need to ensure its replacement will facilitate transparency in order not to lose any further ground in meeting its commitment to the Common Standard.

New Zealand missing opportunities to communicate and raise awareness

Both the 2010 peer review and the 2012 mid-term review recommended that New Zealand invest adequate human and financial resources in communicating to the public about the aid programme (OECD, 2011). Contrary to these recommendations, the previous communications strategy was not implemented and the communications resources for IDG have been limited (MFAT, 2014a; Annex A). Furthermore, there has been no survey of public opinion on development and development co-operation in New Zealand since 2007.

New Zealand has developed a strong vision and narrative around its aid programme, and particularly its focus on the Pacific region (Chapter 2). The results and evaluation systems are also now well placed to provide evidence that can be used to communicate to the public and to partners (see above). Kiribati is a good illustration of the development challenges in the Pacific, but also of the potential impact of New Zealand's development co-operation over time in supporting partner countries to meet those challenges.

Taken together, all these factors should enable New Zealand to communicate a very strong message about its development co-operation programme. These are opportunities, however, currently being largely overlooked by New Zealand.

New Zealand is now committed to developing a new communications strategy. A better understanding of public opinion would be useful to inform this new strategy and challenge any assumptions. The strategy, in line with lessons identified by the OECD, would also have most impact were it to contain a sharp message, seek to deploy a variety of communication tools, including social media, and be adequately resourced (OECD, 2014b).

Funding towards development education initiatives has been discontinued in New Zealand, despite the acknowledged need to build a broader public understanding of the development challenges faced by Pacific nations. New Zealand could draw on NGOs, development experts, the diaspora community and other partners to support the awareness raising effort. As with other DAC members, the ministry could collaborate with the Ministry of Education to enhance the treatment of development and global issues in the school curriculum. This should help build stronger public engagement with official development assistance.

Notes

1. See pages 10-13 of the Strategic Plan (MFAT, 2012) for a list of the global development results and direct New Zealand development results.

2. The 2013-14 Annual Report sets a target of improving on the baseline of % indicators that are on track at the global development results and headline results levels of the New Zealand Aid Programme Strategic Results Framework; they were 55% and 75% respectively in 2013/14.

3. New Zealand Aid Programme evaluates at three interconnected levels, as set out in its evaluation policy:

   i) Strategic evaluations: include policy, sector, process and thematic evaluations. These evaluations are led by the Evaluation and Research Team.

   ii) Programme evaluations: cover one or more of the 26 programmes in the New Zealand Aid Programme framework. Each programme is evaluated once every two programme strategy cycles (six to ten years depending on the length of the programme strategic framework). These evaluations are led by the relevant programme teams with assistance from the Evaluation and Research team.

   iii) Activity evaluations: cover one or more of the aid activities within a programme. All activities to which the New Zealand Aid Programme contributes NZD 10 million or more must be evaluated either during implementation and/or after completion. This evaluation may be commissioned by the New Zealand Aid Programme, by the implementing partner or jointly, provided that minimum quality standards are met. Activity managers lead the management of activity evaluations.

4. See: www.aid.govt.nz/about-aid-programme/measuring-results/evaluation/strategic-evaluation-work-programme-and-reports/eva.

5. The Development Leadership Team provides "thought leadership, people leadership and high-level governance of the New Zealand Aid Programme to ensure effective and efficient delivery" (MFAT, 2014a).

6. Examples include:

   - USAID - COCAR - Coffee rehabilitation: Partner USAID – http://pdf.usaid.gov/pdf_docs/pdacx381.pdf
   - Supporting anti-corruption in the Pacific (Transparency International Secretariat): Partner Australian Department of Foreign Affairs and Trade (DFAT). A summary and full report can be found on the New Zealand Aid Programme website: www.aid.govt.nz/about-aid-programme/measuring-results/evaluation/evaluation-reports/2014-0.
   - Small Business Enterprise Centre (SBEC) Partner: Government of Samoa – being evaluated at present.
   - Private Sector Support Facility (PSSF) Partner: Government of Samoa – being evaluated at present.

7. See: www.aid.govt.nz/funding-and-contracts/research-funds.

Bibliography

Government sources

MFAT (2014a), *OECD Development Assistance Committee Peer Review: Memorandum of New Zealand, Ministry of Foreign Affairs and Trade, Wellington.*

MFAT (2014b), *Annual Report 2013/14*, Ministry of Foreign Affairs and Trade, Wellington, http://mfat.govt.nz/Media-and-publications/Publications/Annual-report/index.php.

MFAT (2014c), *Evaluation Policy for the New Zealand Aid Programme*, Ministry of Foreign Affairs and Trade, Wellington, www.aid.govt.nz/sites/default/files/Evaluation%20Policy.pdf.

MFAT (2014d), *Evaluating Donor Support for Tax Reform in the Pacific*, Taxation Reform Evaluation Factsheet June 2014, Ministry of Foreign Affairs and Trade, Wellington, www.aid.govt.nz/sites/default/files/Taxation%20Reform%20Evaluation%20Fact%20Sheet.pdf.

MFAT (2014e), *What Can We Learn from Activity Evaluations?* Ministry of Foreign Affairs and Trade, Wellington.

MFAT (2013a), *Ten Years of New Zealand Contribution to Peace and Development in Solomon Islands*, Ministry of Foreign Affairs and Trade, Wellington, www.aid.govt.nz/webfm_send/487.

MFAT (2013b), *Strategic Evaluation of Police Work Funded under the New Zealand Aid Programme 2005-2011*, Ministry of Foreign Affairs and Trade, Wellington, www.aid.govt.nz/webfm_send/519.

MFAT (2013c), *Knowledge and Results Five Year Strategy 2013/14 – 2017/18*, Ministry of Foreign Affairs and Trade, Wellington.

MFAT (2012), *Development that Delivers: New Zealand Aid Programme Strategic Plan 2012-15*, Ministry of Foreign Affairs and Trade, Wellington, www.aid.govt.nz/webfm_send/448.

MFAT (2011), Guideline: Developing a Results Framework for a Joint Commitment for Development, Ministry of Foreign Affairs and Trade, Wellington, http://www.aid.govt.nz/sites/default/files/Developing%20a%20Results%20Framework%20for%20a%20Joint%20Commitment%20for%20Development%20guideline.pdf.

Office of the Auditor General (2014), *Annual Report 2013/14*, Audit New Zealand, Wellington, http://mfat.govt.nz/Media-and-publications/Publications/Annual-report/17-Independent-Auditors-Report.php.

Other sources

OECD (2014a), *Measuring and Managing Results in Development Co-operation: A Review of Challenges and Practices among DAC Members and Observers*, OECD, Paris, www.oecd.org/dac/peer-reviews/Measuring-and-managing-results-in-development-co-operation.pdf.

OECD (2014), *Engaging with the Public: Twelve Lessons from DAC Peer Reviews*, OECD Development Co-operation Peer Reviews, OECD Publishing, Paris.
DOI: http://dx.doi.org/10.1787/9789264226739-en.

OECD (2011), *OECD Development Assistance Peer Reviews: New Zealand 2010*, OECD Publishing, Paris, http://dx.doi.org/10.1787/9789264112520-en.

OECD (1991), *Principles for Evaluation of Development Assistance*, Development Assistance Committee, OECD, Paris, www.oecd.org/development/evaluation/2755284.pdf.

Publish What You Fund (2014), "Aid transparency index", www.publishwhatyoufund.org.

Government sources

[illegible]

[illegible]

[illegible]

[illegible], Ministry of Foreign Affairs and Trade, Wellington.

MFAT (2014), [illegible], Ministry of Foreign Affairs and Trade, Wellington.

MFAT (2014), [illegible] of New Zealand [illegible], Ministry of Foreign Affairs and Trade, Wellington.

[illegible]

[illegible]

[illegible]

[illegible]

Other sources

OECD (2014), [illegible]

OECD (201[illegible]), [illegible] DAC [illegible], OECD Publishing, Paris.

OECD (2014), [illegible]

OECD (2014), [illegible]

[illegible] (2014), [illegible]

Chapter 7: New Zealand's humanitarian assistance

Strategic framework

Indicator: Clear political directives and strategies for resilience, response and recovery

New Zealand's aid is focused on the Pacific – the region where New Zealand can clearly add most value – and this also guides its humanitarian policy. New Zealand's approach to recovery and resilience is also built on its comparative advantage, leveraging domestic experience in reducing disaster and climate risks to help design and implement resilience programmes in the Pacific, and closely linking disaster recovery to existing bilateral programmes. However, New Zealand remains a small humanitarian donor, both in absolute volume and in percentage of total ODA; there is scope for more effort in this area.

A clear focus on the Pacific, building on comparative advantage

New Zealand's disaster risk reduction and humanitarian policy (MFAT, 2012a) and cross-government guiding principles for humanitarian assistance in the Pacific (New Zealand Government, 2012) clearly outline a Pacific focus for the humanitarian programme, building on New Zealand 's comparative advantage in the region. The policy also includes a commitment to drawing on Pacific experience to inform global humanitarian dialogue. The policy documents recognise the *Principles and Good Practice of Humanitarian Donorship* (GHD, 2003) and relevant international humanitarian principles and law; this is good practice. The finalisation of these policies meets the recommendation of the 2010 peer review (OECD, 2011).

Working through development programmes to support recovery in the Pacific

The Pacific focus provides useful opportunities for New Zealand to support recovery from disasters, which are the predominant humanitarian concern in that region. Bilateral development funding, also focused on the Pacific (Chapter 2), can be repositioned for recovery programmes when disasters strike, for example to support recovery from severe flooding in the Solomon Islands in 2014. These recovery funds are managed by New Zealand's development teams on the ground, leveraging existing knowledge and networks. This, in turn, allows New Zealand to tailor its recovery programmes to the context, enabling, for example, a bold decision to provide budget support to Samoa to help fund recovery from the 2009 tsunami. Outside of the Pacific, NGOs can apply for 12-month funding for recovery programmes.

Effectively leveraging domestic experience to boost resilience to disasters and climate change

New Zealand's experience as a disaster-prone nation has given rise to a strong commitment to boosting resilience in partner countries, especially to disaster and climate change risks. Important lessons from domestic disasters, most recently the 2011 Christchurch earthquake, are actively shared with multilateral partners, who are in turn urged to better integrate disaster risk reduction aspects across their programmes. In the bilateral programme, the focus is on developing national and regional response capacity, using both humanitarian and development funding, and capitalising on expertise across government.[1] Bilateral resilience programmes usually incorporate a long-term perspective, including promoting partner country government prioritisation of, and budget allocations for, risk reduction. Other donors could clearly learn from New Zealand's approach to risk reduction programming. However, partners, especially NGOs, find it harder to make the case for funding for their own disaster risk reduction projects; it is notable that only 4% of the Partnerships Fund (Chapter 5) is allocated for this purpose.

A small donor, with scope to increase its budget volume

The peer review team heard strong political support for humanitarian programming in New Zealand. Despite this backing, the humanitarian budget remains quite modest, standing at USD 29.19 million in 2013.[2] The percentage of ODA allocated to humanitarian assistance for that year was also modest, at 7.9%; 14 DAC members allocate more than 8% for humanitarian programming, with 8 of these allocating more than 10% of their total ODA.[3] This clearly leaves scope for further budgetary effort, especially if New Zealand moves to increase its overall ODA envelope (Chapter 3).

Effective programme design

Indicator: Programmes target the highest risk to life and livelihood

There is good use of bilateral colleagues in the Pacific to provide early warning information, which can then be used to drive early funding decisions. Partners are actively encouraged to include the voice of affected populations in programme design and implementation. However, and despite the Pacific focus of the programme, actual funding allocations are split between the Pacific and the rest of the world; it is unclear how New Zealand chooses where to fund for these non-Pacific allocations. In addition, New Zealand's criteria for funding decisions are very broad, and decisions are made at a political level; this risks creating misperceptions about the principled, objective nature of funding allocations.

Broad criteria for funding decisions; actual allocations not fully aligned with the primary focus of NZ policy

Given the size of the humanitarian budget, it is useful that New Zealand has chosen to primarily focus on an area where it can clearly add value, i.e. the Pacific.[4] Focusing the humanitarian programme supports good practices such as division of labour on burden sharing, ensuring that funding decisions are of sufficient scale to justify the administrative burden for partners and staff, and allowing a small humanitarian team to monitor and add value to each and every funding decision.

However, in 2013, only 59% of New Zealand's bilateral budget allocations were for the Pacific, i.e. Oceania (36%) and the Philippines (23%); the remainder went to other crises. New Zealand defends this allocation pattern by citing its moral obligation as a good global citizen, and noting that crisis responses in the Pacific are typically less costly, leaving funds for other humanitarian emergencies. The 2010 peer review asked New Zealand to clarify its rational for engaging in global response; the new policy says that New Zealand will support the co-ordinated action of the international community, and use its domestic and Pacific experience to inform global policy dialogue (MFAT, 2012). However, how New Zealand chooses to do this – how it chooses which crises to fund beyond the Pacific – remains to be shown.

New Zealand states that individual humanitarian allocation decisions are made through ministerial submissions, drawn up as and when crises occur (MFAT, 2014). These ministerial decisions should be based on the criteria outlined in the humanitarian policy,[5] or perhaps based on an objective assessment of where New Zealand can add most value. However the policy criteria are so broad that almost any crisis could be considered. If New Zealand wants to avoid the risk of misperceptions about the principled, objective nature of its funding allocations, it might consider tighter allocation criteria and the publication of the rationale behind individual funding decisions.

Good use of bilateral colleagues to provide early warning information

New Zealand invests in early warning systems, matching technical hardware with capacity strengthening and public awareness, and building on traditional knowledge and systems where possible (MFAT, 2014). For its own programming, the humanitarian team relies on early warning of disasters from bilateral colleagues and other sources in the Pacific; this often leads to rapid funding allocations. Partners are, however, concerned that New Zealand – like most other donors – may not be as reactive when it comes to slow onset crises such as droughts, which can also affect the Pacific.

Partners encouraged to listen to affected populations

New Zealand relies on its partners to ensure that affected people have a voice in programme design and delivery; for example by making this part of the criteria for funding from the Disaster Response Partnership. In addition, working with local partners is actively promoted, for example through the Partnerships Fund (Chapter 5). Aid programme staff are also regularly deployed to support Pacific disaster responses; these staff will also help ensure that the voice of affected populations is heard in programme design and delivery.

Effective delivery, partnerships and instruments

Indicator: Delivery modalities and partnerships help deliver quality

New Zealand's clear strength is disaster response, and it has developed effective cross-government mechanisms to ensure rapid and appropriate disaster response in the Pacific, including long-standing co-ordination arrangements with the other major donors in the region. Complex emergencies are largely funded through multi-annual, un-earmarked contributions to the multilateral system, providing these agencies with both predictability and flexibility. There are major barriers to funding NGO work in complex crises; a review of how New Zealand should engage with NGOs in humanitarian assistance could be a useful next step.

Good tools for funding complex emergencies through the multilateral system, but significant barriers for NGOs

Complex emergencies are not a policy priority, but they do receive a major share of New Zealand's humanitarian funding, so it is important that there are the right tools for this part of the programme. In this regard, multilateral partners are well served; receiving multi-annual, largely un-earmarked allocations (Chapter 5). New Zealand also provides funding to the Central Emergency Response Fund – USD 2.4 million in 2015 (UN CERF, 2014) – some of which will also be allocated to forgotten crises.[6] NGOs, however, do not enjoy the same predictability and timeliness of funding now that they must apply through the Partnerships Fund (Chapter 5). In addition, and unlike other OECD/DAC donors, New Zealand will only fund 50% of NGO humanitarian programmes outside the Pacific, with the other 50% expected to come from public donations. This creates significant barriers for NGOs, and increases the risk that funding will be for high-profile crises or issues that capture the public's attention – meaning less emphasis on less "sexy" issues such as disaster risk reduction.

Effective cross-government mechanisms to ensure rapid and appropriate disaster response in the Pacific

Disaster response is clearly New Zealand's key strength in humanitarian assistance. There are useful tools for funding partners, most notably the Disaster Response Partnership, which provides rapidly disbursed six-month funding to 16 pre-accredited NGOs,[7] supplemented by arrangements with various partners to pre-position emergency supplies in the Pacific and in Southeast Asia. However, the bulk of New Zealand's disaster response is bilateral, building on existing expertise across government. It is co-ordinated through an Emergency Task Force using standard operating procedures that closely mirror the way those teams work together in domestic crises. Other countries could learn from

New Zealand's Emergency Task Force arrangements. Not only is this body cross-government,[8] but it also interacts with France and Australia, the other two first-line responders in the Pacific, and has NGO and New Zealand Red Cross members. This broad range of stakeholders necessitates discipline and a clear definition of roles; New Zealand is committed to this as well as learning from past experiences. Regular simulations and other preparedness exercises help build cohesion.

Support provided to disaster-affected countries varies with the context, often informed by New Zealand's development personnel on the ground. New Zealand can provide backup staff to support partner country National Disaster Management Offices and/or to support overworked colleagues in country offices, as well as in-kind relief supplies and other support. Medical support is one specialist area, building on existing networks with health professionals and institutions across the Pacific; these pre-existing contacts help ensure that the response is appropriate for the context. Medical assistance teams were also recently deployed for the Cyclone Haiyan response, and at the time of this peer review, medical volunteers were being recruited to support the Ebola response in Sierra Leone.

A constructive and useful partner to multilateral agencies; the rationale and strategy for engagement with NGOs is less clear

As noted above, New Zealand is a good partner to United Nations agencies and funds, and to the International Committee of the Red Cross. Multilateral partners have been carefully chosen based on their ability to provide effective responses; here New Zealand will work to influence continued improvement through participation on governing boards, while minimising the administrative burden by providing multi-annual, largely un-earmarked funds and accepting standard agency reports. These partners are universally positive about their relationship with New Zealand. However, relationships with NGOs – as for development programmes (Chapter 5) – are more complicated. There is a Disaster Relief Forum,[9] where operational and policy issues are discussed three times a year; partners would like more policy engagement. Providing additional clarity to NGOs about funding decisions could also be useful, to avoid potential misperceptions that funding decisions are made at a political level. Overall, If New Zealand wishes to continue to engage with NGOs in the humanitarian programme, it could be useful to review the rationale for that engagement, define what role NGOs should play in delivering an effective response, and how New Zealand will support that work.

Active, long-standing donor co-ordination in the Pacific

There is active, and long-standing, donor co-ordination in the Pacific through the FRANZ mechanism, grouping the three main donors: France, Australia and New Zealand.[10] This group includes civilian and military actors, and now also involves the Red Cross movement and the United Nations. Chaired on a rotational basis, it meets to plan for upcoming Pacific disaster seasons and then receives and responds to requests from affected countries. New Zealand also actively engages with FRANZ members, plus Japan, the European Union and the United States, on disaster risk reduction programming in both the Pacific, and through the ASEAN regional body.

Organisation fit for purpose

Indicator: Systems, structures, processes and people work together effectively and efficiently

Collaboration on disaster response across government, under the ministry's leadership, builds on lessons from working together in domestic crises, most recently the 2011 Christchurch earthquake. Other donors could learn from this system. Civil-military principles are actively promoted. Humanitarian staff have a heavy workload due to New Zealand's hands-on disaster response model, but also with the preparation of individual funding decisions. Increasing delegation of authority for funding decisions could usefully free up staff time for more policy reflection, and enable New Zealand to share some of its good practice with other donors and partners, especially in the lead-up to the World Humanitarian Summit in 2016.

Effective whole-of-government collaboration

The Emergency Task Force, under ministry leadership, is the key cross-government co-ordination mechanism. The mechanism involves a broad range of stakeholders, adapted to the particular emergency context. As might be expected, there have been some challenges in merging the response protocols and operating procedures used by different government actors, but these issues are being worked out, often during responses to domestic crises. The peer team heard that, overall, the mechanism functions effectively.

Raising awareness of civil military principles

In line with the commitment to international principles in the humanitarian policy (MFAT, 2012a), all New Zealand humanitarian responses are civilian-led. To reinforce understanding of the civilian character of responses, and to ensure that key military personnel are aware of relevant civil military guidance, New Zealand carries out briefings with military personnel prior to international deployments. In 2013, a useful civil-military workshop was held in the Pacific, bringing together Pacific government representatives, military personnel and NGOs. Domestically, the NGO umbrella body, the Council for International Development, is funded to provide civil-military training for NGOs, military and police personnel, and ministry staff.

Heavy workload from the hands-on operational model and limited delegation of authority

Since the last peer review, the ministry has consolidated its humanitarian staff into one team, and also provided training to staff who could be co-opted to support major disaster responses, thereby increasing the pool of humanitarian expertise across the ministry. The core team of six may seem quite large for a donor of this size, but the day-to-day workload is high. This is because of the limited delegation of authority – much time is taken up preparing briefing notes to inform funding decisions – and because of the largely operational response model, supporting bilateral response teams across the Pacific. Clearly the operational response model is an effective way for New Zealand to respond to disasters, and so this workload driver will continue into the future. However, increasing delegation of authority for funding decisions could usefully free up staff time for more policy reflection, and enable New Zealand to share some of its good practice with other donors and partners, especially in the lead-up to the World Humanitarian Summit in 2016.

Results, learning and accountability

Indicator: Results are measured and communicated, and lessons learnt

New Zealand reports annually on its performance against strategic priorities, but the reports that are made public are more anecdotal in nature, and provide little on impact or results. There are systematic after-action reviews of the bilateral disaster responses, supplemented by a major review at the end of each Pacific cyclone season; the results of these reviews are translated into learning for future operations. The competitive nature of funding provides a disincentive for partners to share learning, however, and there is not yet strategic guidance on when and how humanitarian programmes should be evaluated.

Regular performance reports

It is standard New Zealand government practice to set out expected results and to assess progress on a regular basis. Accordingly, there is an annual report on progress against humanitarian priorities (MFAT, 2014). This is an internal report. It would be useful to make it public, promoting accountability against set targets.

Systematic after-action reviews, but no culture of monitoring and learning with partners

Bilateral disaster responses are often subject to after-action debriefs, and the bilateral programme is systematically reviewed after each cyclone season (MFAT, 2014). The results from these operational reviews are used to improve future responses, and to help harmonise working practices across government.

In the Pacific, monitoring of partner programmes is conducted by staff in country offices, or by staff who are deployed from Wellington to support disaster responses, where this is feasible. This applies mostly to NGO partners since multilateral agencies, who mostly work outside the Pacific, cannot be actively monitored. Lessons are not actively shared between partners; this may be because the competitive basis of the NGO funding system reduces the incentive to share learning.

New Zealand has not yet determined a strategy for using evaluation in its humanitarian programme, although the peer team heard that options for this are being considered.

Communication of activities but not results

New Zealand publishes an annual *Year in Review* report that includes humanitarian aspects,[11] but this is more a newsletter than a statement of results. Still, it does serve the purpose of informing taxpayers and other stakeholders about the activities and partners that have been funded under the humanitarian programme.

Notes

1. The government departments involved in disaster resilience programming include the New Zealand Defence Force, the Ministry of Civil Defence and Emergency Management and the New Zealand Fire Service.

2. Source: OECD Creditor Reporting System, 2013 figures, commitments in current prices (OECD, 2013).

3. Belgium, Canada, Finland, Ireland, Luxembourg, Switzerland, the United Kingdom and the United States all allocated more than 10% of their ODA to humanitarian assistance in 2013.

4. New Zealand's aid policy states "given New Zealand's strong cultural and political ties, and its geographic proximity, Pacific Island countries in south-west and central Pacific are the primary focus of our humanitarian assistance and investments in disaster risk reduction" (MFAT, 2012).

5. These criteria include the issuance of a humanitarian appeal, the scale of need, the nature of the crisis (with priority given to rapid onset or rapidly deteriorating crises), existing relationships with countries, the possibility for a whole-of-government approach and relevant knowledge of crises, appropriate response mechanisms, and capacity to respond (MFAT, 2012).

6. Funding to the CERF is un-earmarked, but the CERF allocates around one-third of the funding it receives to forgotten crises.

7. New Zealand's humanitarian policy states that partners will be selected based on their commitment to humanitarian principles and standards, and on their ability to deliver effective and efficient assistance that has impact and promotes sustainability where this is relevant (MFAT, 2012).

8. The Emergency Task Force includes personnel from the Department of Prime Minister and Cabinet, New Zealand Defence Force, Police, Ministry of Health, Ministry of Pacific Island Affairs, the Ministry of Civil Defence and Emergency Management, and the New Zealand Fire Service. It may also call in other Ministries as required. More at www.aid.govt.nz/where-we-work/emergencies-developing-countries.

9. The Disaster Relief Forum is a standing committee of the Council for International Development.

10. The FRANZ mechanism was established in 1992.

11. The 2013 Year in Review report is available at www.aid.govt.nz/webfm_send/552 .

Bibliography

Government sources

MFAT (2014), *OECD Development Assistance Committee Peer Review: Memorandum of New Zealand,* Ministry of Foreign Affairs and Trade, Wellington.

MFAT (2012), *Policies and Strategies for Humanitarian Assistance and Disaster Risk Reduction,* Ministry of Foreign Affairs and Trade, Wellington, www.aid.govt.nz/webfm_send/319.

New Zealand Government (2012), *10 Guiding Principles for the Provision of Humanitarian Assistance in the Pacific,* New Zealand Government, Wellington, www.aid.govt.nz/webfm_send/335.

Other sources

International Meeting on Good Humanitarian Donorship (2003), *The Principles and Good Practice of Humanitarian Donorship,* declaration signed in Stockholm, 16-17 June 2003, www.ifrc.org/Docs/idrl/I267EN.pdf.

OECD (2013), Creditor Reporting System Aid Activity (database), http://dx.doi.org/10.1787/dev-data-en.

OECD (2011), *OECD Development Assistance Peer Reviews: New Zealand 2010*, OECD Publishing, Paris, http://dx.doi.org/10.1787/9789264112520-en.

UN CERF (2014), *CERF Pledges and Contributions: As of 14 April 2014*, United Nations Central Emergency Response Fund, United Nations, Washington DC, https://docs.unocha.org/sites/dms/CERF/CERF Pledges and Contributions 2006 - 2014 as of 14 April 2014.pdf.

Annex A: Progress since the 2010 DAC peer review recommendations

Key Issues: Development beyond aid

Recommendations 2010	Progress on implementation
Continue to develop whole-of-government frameworks, agreed with partner countries, to ensure stronger oversight of all activities implemented by New Zealand departments in these countries.	**Partially implemented**
Set and monitor inter-departmental targets with agreed indicators in priority areas of domestic and foreign policies to further promote development concerns.	**Not implemented**

Key Issues: Strategic orientations

Recommendations 2010	Progress on implementation
Clarify the new strategic orientations of the aid programme and develop a medium-term strategy explaining the government's approach to economic development to reduce poverty, while recognising the importance of the environmental and social dimensions of sustainable development.	**Implemented**
Adopt a more strategic and systematic approach to cross-cutting issues, including disaster risk management and climate change, backed up with appropriate systems and resources, and clear connections between development and humanitarian activities.	**Partially implemented**

Key Issues: Aid volume, channels and allocations

Recommendations 2010	Progress on implementation
Work towards increasing its official aid to meet the UN target of 0.7% ODA/GNI. A first step could be to develop a clear and strategic forward spending plan setting out an intermediate target and a timeline for achieving it.	**Not implemented**
Further reduce geographic dispersion by clearly defining its comparative advantage and setting out priorities for programming. In doing so, New Zealand should ensure new arrangements on division of labour are developed following the principles agreed in the Accra Agenda for Action.	**Implemented**
Replicate its good practice on predictability for bilateral and regional programming by making multi-year commitments to its priority multilateral partners.	**Implemented**

Key Issues: Organisation and management

Recommendations 2010	Progress on implementation
Complete the MFAT's organisational change process. In re-integrating the aid programme, the ministry should build on its strengths while recognising its specificity and its related needs, in particular as regards development expertise capacity.	**Implemented**
Finish adjusting IDG's business model to the new aid mandate to enable it to continue to deliver a growing aid programme efficiently and with more effective delegation of authority to country offices. This requires IDG to equip posts with appropriate capability, streamline its aid management systems and clarify functions and lines of accountability.	**Partially implemented**
Maintain a core cadre of development professionals and reinforce workforce and training planning to ensure IDG has the right skills mix. IDG should also consider options for widening the role of local staff, while ensuring that their added value is recognised in the ministry.	**Partially implemented**

Key Issues: Delivery and partnerships

Recommendations 2010	Progress on implementation
Develop a strategic approach to the private sector and research institutes to implement the new orientations of the aid programme. IDG should plan a review of the way it engages with NGOs at headquarters and in the field, and ensure it makes the most of synergies between the aid programme and NGOs.	**Partially implemented**
Promote broader understanding and dedication to aid effectiveness within the ministry and other government departments, and set out a more systematic approach to implementation which is binding for all relevant government departments.	**Partially implemented**
Continue to move towards greater use of programme-based approaches and budget support, equipping itself to handle the different accountabilities and risks associated with these types of modalities and ensuring appropriate training and guidance.	**Partially implemented**
Explore ways to provide rolling three-year resource indications in order to make its aid more predictable in the medium term in line with its Accra commitments.	**Implemented**
Promote understanding of capacity development across government and beyond, and assess the range of tools at its disposal and their contribution to capacity development.	**Not examined**

Key Issues: Results management and accountability

Recommendations 2010	Progress on implementation
Update its development co-operation communication strategy and maintain dedicated resources to promote the policy statement and communicate results.	**Not implemented**
Build on positive efforts for managing for results and knowledge sharing to develop a more strategic use of monitoring and evaluation for forward-looking management.	**Partially implemented**

Key Issues: Humanitarian assistance

Recommendations 2010	Progress on implementation
Clarify its rationale for engaging in both global response and policy debates, and how these are linked and mutually supportive.	**Partially implemented**
Increase the level of humanitarian specialist expertise in the Pacific and Global humanitarian teams and review its humanitarian policy.	**Implemented**

Figure A.1 New Zealand's implementation of 2010 peer review recommendations

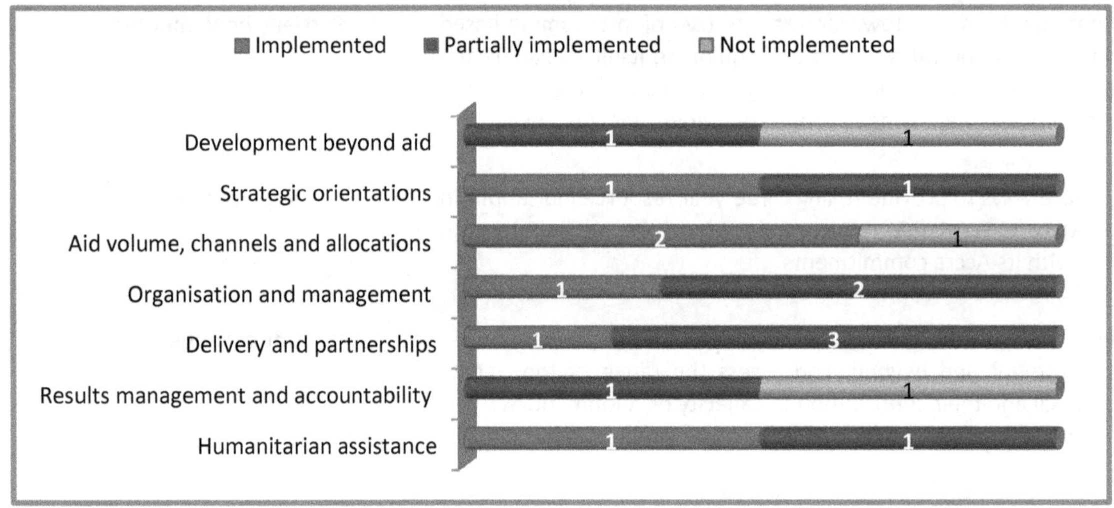

Annex B: OECD/DAC standard suite of tables

Table B.1 Total financial flows

USD million at current prices and exchange rates

New Zealand	1999-2003	2004-2008	2009	2010	2011	2012	2013
					Net disbursements		
Total official flows	130	290	317	351	434	460	468
Official development assistance	129	282	309	342	424	449	457
Bilateral	98	222	226	271	330	362	351
Multilateral	31	60	83	71	95	88	107
Other official flows	1	7	8	8	10	11	11
Bilateral	1	7	8	8	10	11	11
Multilateral	-	-	-	-	-	-	-
Net Private Grants	15	54	46	49	74	134	76
Private flows at market terms	18	26	24	26	28	35	37
Bilateral: *of which*	18	26	24	26	28	35	37
Direct investment	18	26	24	26	28	35	37
Export credits	-	-	-	-	-	-	-
Multilateral	-	-	-	-	-	-	-
Total flows	163	370	387	426	536	629	581
for reference:							
ODA (at constant 2012 USD million)	278	376	424	391	431	449	441
ODA (as a % of GNI)	0.24	0.27	0.28	0.26	0.28	0.28	0.26
Total flows (as a % of GNI) (a)	0.31	0.35	0.35	0.32	0.35	0.39	0.33
ODA to and channelled through NGOs							
- In USD million	10	44	24	42	57	48	86
- In percentage of total net ODA	7	16	8	12	13	11	19
- DAC countries' average % of total net ODA	8	8	7	8	9	13	13

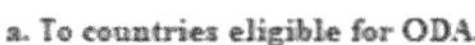

a. To countries eligible for ODA.

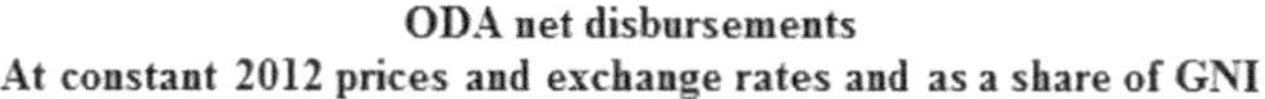

ODA net disbursements
At constant 2012 prices and exchange rates and as a share of GNI

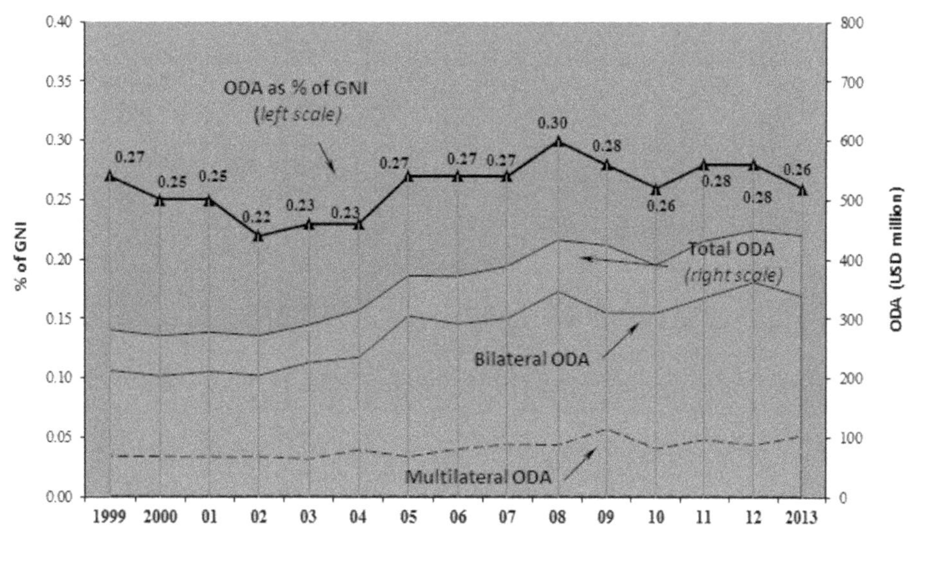

Table B.2 ODA by main categories

Disbursements

New Zealand	Constant 2012 USD million					Per cent share of gross disbursements					Total DAC 2012%
	2009	2010	2011	2012	2013	2009	2010	2011	2012	2013	
Gross Bilateral ODA	**310**	**310**	**335**	**362**	**338**	**73**	**79**	**78**	**81**	**77**	**73**
Budget support	-	50	39	49	53	-	13	9	11	12	2
of which: General budget support	15	19	16	18	15	3	5	4	4	3	1
Core contributions & pooled prog.& funds	-	73	74	58	47	-	19	17	13	11	13
of which: Core support to national NGOs	25	9	8	6	7	6	2	2	1	2	1
Core support to international NGOs	8	11	7	9	10	2	3	2	2	2	1
Core support to PPPs	0	0	0	0	0	0	0	0	0	0	0
Project-type interventions	-	64	97	112	97	-	16	22	25	22	41
of which: Investment projects	21	12	36	41	33	5	3	8	9	8	11
Experts and other technical assistance	-	43	38	46	40	-	11	9	10	9	4
Scholarships and student costs in donor countries	-	27	28	33	39	-	7	6	7	9	2
of which: Imputed student costs	-	-	-	-	-	-	-	-	-	-	2
Debt relief grants	-	-	-	-	-	-	-	-	-	-	2
Administrative costs	33	37	46	43	42	8	9	11	10	10	5
Other in-donor expenditures	16	16	14	20	19	4	4	3	4	4	3
of which: refugees in donor countries	13	14	14	19	19						
Gross Multilateral ODA	**114**	**81**	**96**	**88**	**103**	**27**	**21**	**22**	**19**	**23**	**27**
UN agencies	60	41	46	47	46	14	10	11	10	10	5
EU institutions	-	-	-	-	-	-	-	-	-	-	9
World Bank group	16	14	16	2	30	4	3	4	1	7	6
Regional development banks	8	-	17	16	8	2	-	4	4	2	3
Other multilateral	31	27	18	23	19	7	7	4	5	4	5
Total gross ODA	**424**	**391**	**431**	**449**	**441**	**100**	**100**	**100**	**100**	**100**	**100**
Repayments and debt cancellation	-	-	-	-	-						
Total net ODA	**424**	**391**	**431**	**449**	**441**						
For reference:											
Free standing technical co-operation	*72*	*71*	*65*	*79*	*79*						
Net debt relief	-	-	-	-	-						

Contributions to UN Agencies (2012-13 Average)

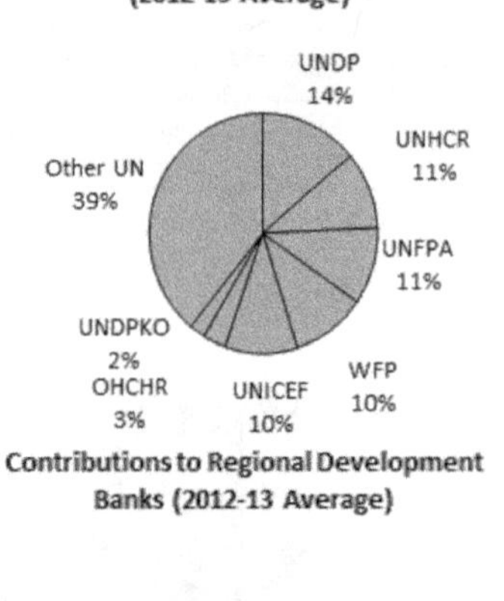

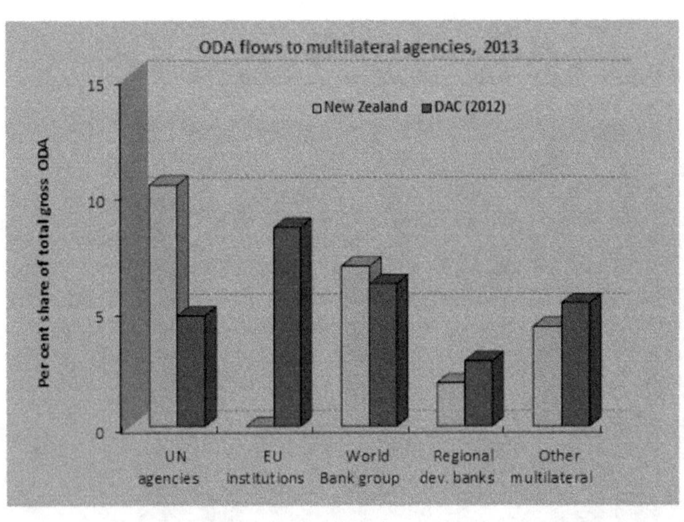

Contributions to Regional Development Banks (2012-13 Average)

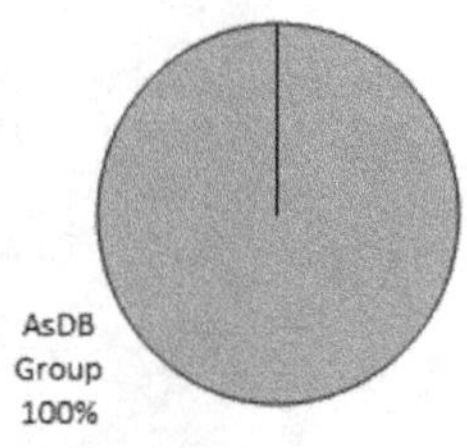

Table B.3 Bilateral ODA allocable by region and income group

Gross disbursements

New Zealand	Constant 2012 USD million					Per cent share					Total DAC
	2009	2010	2011	2012	2013	2009	2010	2011	2012	2013	2012%
Africa	13	12	15	7	4	5	5	5	2	1	43
Sub-Saharan Africa	13	12	14	6	4	5	5	5	2	1	37
North Africa	-	-	1	1	0	-	-	0	0	0	4
Asia	58	50	64	73	62	22	19	22	23	22	34
South and Central Asia	17	11	14	22	11	6	4	5	7	4	20
Far East	40	40	50	51	51	15	15	17	16	18	14
America	6	6	4	2	2	2	2	1	1	1	10
North and Central America	2	3	1	1	1	1	1	0	0	0	4
South America	3	3	3	1	1	1	1	1	0	1	5
Middle East	2	2	3	3	4	1	1	1	1	1	7
Oceania	186	195	209	228	214	70	73	71	73	75	2
Europe	-	-	0	-	-	-	-	0	-	-	3
Total bilateral allocable by region	265	266	295	313	286	100	100	100	100	100	100
Least developed	113	95	94	118	105	54	44	40	48	47	41
Other low-income	2	5	2	1	2	1	2	1	1	1	4
Lower middle-income	75	82	99	95	91	36	38	42	38	40	36
Upper middle-income	19	34	40	34	27	9	16	17	14	12	18
More advanced developing countries	0	0	-	-	-	0	0	-	-	-	-
Total bilateral allocable by income	210	217	236	249	225	100	100	100	100	100	100
For reference:											
Total bilateral	310	310	335	362	338	*100*	*100*	*100*	*100*	*100*	*100*
of which: Unallocated by region	*45*	*44*	*40*	*48*	*51*	*14*	*14*	*12*	*13*	*15*	*24*
of which: Unallocated by income	*100*	*92*	*99*	*113*	*113*	*32*	*30*	*30*	*31*	*33*	*32*

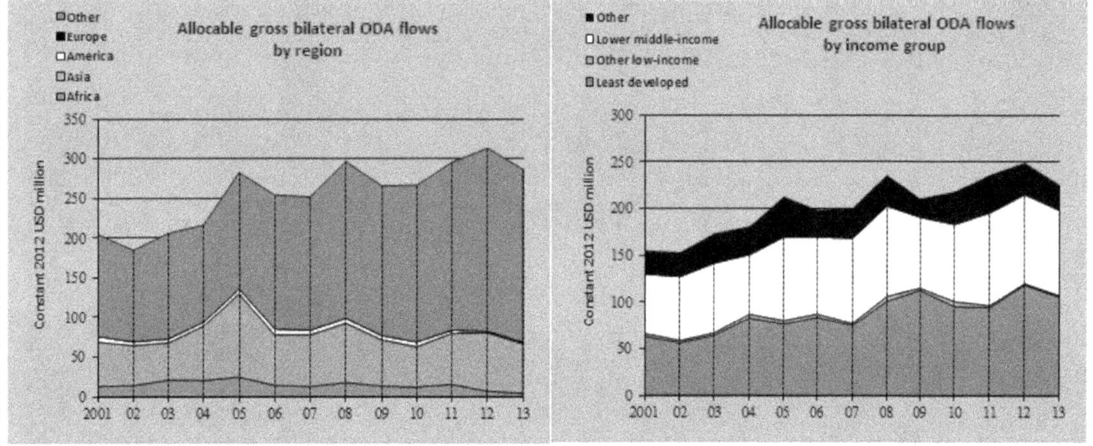

1. Each region includes regional amounts which cannot be allocated by sub-region. The sum of the sub-regional amounts may therefore fall short of the regional total.

Table B.4 Main recipients of bilateral ODA

Gross disbursements

New Zealand	2002-06 average			Memo:		2007-11 average			Memo:		2012-13 average			Memo:
				DAC					*DAC*					*DAC*
	Current USD million	Constant 2012 USD mln	Per cent share	*countries' average %*		Current USD million	Constant 2012 USD mln	Per cent share	*countries' average %*		Current USD million	Constant 2012 USD mln	Per cent share	*countries' average %*
Solomon Islands	10	15	6		Solomon Islands	23	27	8		Solomon Islands	32	31	9	
Niue	9	14	6		Papua New Guinea	19	22	7		Papua New Guinea	22	21	6	
Papua New Guinea	9	14	6		Tokelau	15	17	5		Tokelau	20	20	6	
Tokelau	8	13	5		Niue	13	15	5		Samoa	20	20	6	
Indonesia	8	12	5		Vanuatu	12	14	4		Tonga	16	16	5	
Top 5 recipients	**44**	**68**	**27**	**50**	**Top 5 recipients**	**81**	**96**	**30**	**36**	**Top 5 recipients**	**110**	**108**	**31**	**35**
Samoa	5	9	3		Samoa	11	13	4		Vanuatu	15	15	4	
Afghanistan	5	8	3		Indonesia	10	12	4		Niue	13	13	4	
Vanuatu	5	8	3		Tonga	10	12	4		Afghanistan	12	12	3	
Tonga	4	7	3		Cook Islands	7	8	3		Cook Islands	12	11	3	
Cook Islands	4	6	2		Vietnam	6	8	2		Kiribati	10	10	3	
Top 10 recipients	**68**	**106**	**42**	**68**	**Top 10 recipients**	**126**	**149**	**47**	**51**	**Top 10 recipients**	**170**	**167**	**48**	**49**
Iraq	4	6	2		Timor-Leste	6	7	2		Indonesia	9	9	3	
Fiji	4	6	2		Kiribati	5	6	2		Vietnam	9	9	3	
Philippines	3	5	2		Afghanistan	5	6	2		Timor-Leste	9	9	2	
Timor-Leste	3	5	2		Cambodia	4	5	2		Philippines	7	7	2	
Cambodia	3	4	2		Fiji	4	4	1		Fiji	6	6	2	
Top 15 recipients	**84**	**132**	**52**	**76**	**Top 15 recipients**	**150**	**177**	**55**	**55**	**Top 15 recipients**	**210**	**206**	**59**	**56**
Vietnam	3	4	2		Philippines	3	4	1		Laos	5	5	1	
Sudan	2	3	1		Tuvalu	3	3	1		Tuvalu	4	4	1	
Kiribati	2	3	1		Laos	2	3	1		Cambodia	4	4	1	
China	2	2	1		Zimbabwe	2	2	1		Nauru	2	2	1	
Laos	1	2	1		Nepal	2	2	1		Syria	2	2	1	
Top 20 recipients	**94**	**147**	**58**	**80**	**Top 20 recipients**	**162**	**191**	**60**	**58**	**Top 20 recipients**	**227**	**223**	**64**	**60**
Total (111 recipients)	116	183	72		Total (95 recipients)	186	220	69		Total (73 recipients)	241	237	68	
Unallocated	45	69	28	5	Unallocated	85	101	31	24	Unallocated	115	113	32	28
Total bilateral gross	**161**	**252**	**100**	**100**	**Total bilateral gross**	**270**	**320**	**100**	**100**	**Total bilateral gross**	**356**	**350**	**100**	**100**

1. 2012

Table B.5 Bilateral ODA by major purposes

at constant 2011 prices and exchange rates

Gross disbursements - Two-year average

New Zealand	2002-2006 average		2007-11 average		2012-13 average		2012
	2012 USD million	Per cent	2012 USD million	Per cent	2012 USD million	Per cent	Total DAC per cent
Social infrastructure & services	**110**	**48**	**139**	**47**	**146**	**42**	**41**
Education	54	24	60	20	72	21	8
of which: basic education	14	6	23	8	23	7	2
Health	12	5	18	6	21	6	6
of which: basic health	7	3	11	4	12	4	4
Population & reproductive health	4	2	7	2	6	2	7
Water supply & sanitation	3	1	4	1	7	2	6
Government & civil society	28	12	46	15	37	11	12
of which: Conflict, peace & security	2	1	11	4	10	3	3
Other social infrastructure & services	8	4	5	2	3	1	2
Economic infrastructure & services	**8**	**4**	**23**	**8**	**55**	**16**	**17**
Transport & storage	3	1	14	5	29	8	8
Communications	0	0	0	0	1	0	0
Energy	1	1	3	1	17	5	6
Banking & financial services	3	1	2	1	4	1	2
Business & other services	1	0	3	1	5	2	1
Production sectors	**12**	**5**	**22**	**7**	**35**	**10**	**8**
Agriculture, forestry & fishing	7	3	12	4	20	6	6
Industry, mining & construction	1	1	3	1	2	0	1
Trade & tourism	4	2	7	2	13	4	1
Multisector	**11**	**5**	**13**	**4**	**12**	**3**	**10**
Commodity and programme aid	**21**	**9**	**25**	**8**	**17**	**5**	**3**
Action relating to debt	**0**	**0**	-	-	-	-	**3**
Humanitarian aid	**31**	**14**	**29**	**10**	**23**	**7**	**8**
Administrative costs of donors	**20**	**9**	**34**	**11**	**43**	**12**	**6**
Refugees in donor countries	**14**	**6**	**14**	**5**	**19**	**5**	**4**
Total bilateral allocable	**228**	**100**	**298**	**100**	**349**	**100**	**100**
For reference:							
Total bilateral	*252*	*78*	*320*	*77*	*350*	*79*	*58*
of which: Unallocated	*24*	*8*	*22*	*5*	*0*	*0*	*1*
Total multilateral	*71*	*22*	*93*	*23*	*95*	*21*	*42*
Total ODA	***324***	***100***	***414***	***100***	***445***	***100***	***100***

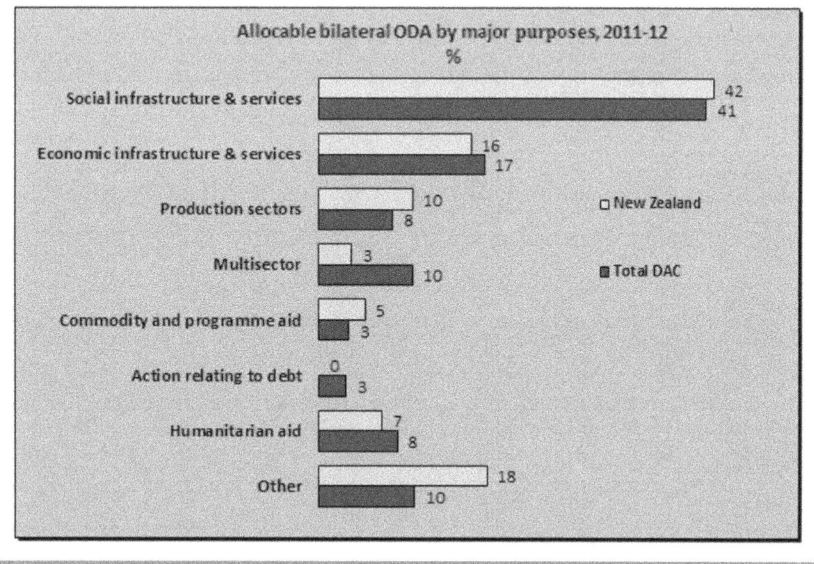

Table B.6 Comparative aid performance

Net disbursements

	Official development assistance			Grant element of ODA (commitments)	Share of multilateral aid				ODA to LDCs Bilateral and through multilateral agencies	
	2012		2006-07 to 2011-12 Average annual % change in real terms	2012	2012				2012	
					% of ODA		% of GNI			
	USD million	% of GNI		% (a)	(b)	(c)	(b)	(c)	% of ODA	% of GNI
Australia	5 403	0.36	7.1	99.8	15.8		0.06		30.3	0.11
Austria	1 106	0.28	-9.5	100.0	51.6	26.7	0.14	0.07	22.0	0.06
Belgium	2 315	0.47	3.0	99.7	38.1	18.7	0.18	0.09	30.4	0.14
Canada	5 650	0.32	3.2	100.0	28.3		0.09		34.4	0.11
Czech Republic	220	0.12	2.9	100.0	69.8	16.2	0.08	0.02	26.7	0.03
Denmark	2 693	0.83	0.4	100.0	28.6	19.7	0.24	0.16	37.3	0.31
Finland	1 320	0.53	5.9	100.0	39.5	25.3	0.21	0.13	33.7	0.18
France	12 028	0.45	2.0	79.5	34.1	16.7	0.15	0.08	21.1	0.10
Germany	12 939	0.37	2.0	88.4	33.7	14.9	0.13	0.06	28.4	0.11
Greece	327	0.13	-6.4	100.0	67.2	4.9	0.09	0.01	15.3	0.02
Iceland	26	0.22	-5.7	100.0	18.8		0.04		45.1	0.10
Ireland	808	0.47	-4.0	100.0	33.7	17.9	0.16	0.08	51.7	0.24
Italy	2 737	0.14	-3.6	99.4	77.2	21.8	0.11	0.03	25.6	0.04
Japan	10 605	0.17	-3.6	88.5	39.6		0.07		43.8	0.08
Korea	1 597	0.14	21.6	94.2	25.9		0.04		36.2	0.05
Luxembourg	399	1.00	0.5	100.0	30.7	22.8	0.31	0.23	36.5	0.37
Netherlands	5 523	0.71	-1.2	100.0	30.2	19.2	0.21	0.14	21.1	0.15
New Zealand	449	0.28	3.0	100.0	19.5		0.05		32.0	0.09
Norway	4 753	0.93	1.7	100.0	25.9		0.24		29.1	0.27
Poland	421	0.09	3.1	..	73.5	5.8	0.07	0.01	18.5	0.02
Portugal	581	0.28	6.8	84.6	31.6	5.1	0.09	0.01	30.4	0.09
Slovak Republic	80	0.09	1.5	100.0	76.2	8.3	0.07	0.01	19.3	0.02
Slovenia	58	0.13	2.0	100.0	67.3	13.8	0.09	0.02	17.3	0.02
Spain	2 037	0.16	-8.3	100.0	51.6	4.6	0.08	0.01	23.7	0.04
Sweden	5 240	0.97	2.3	100.0	30.6	24.0	0.30	0.23	29.4	0.29
Switzerland	3 056	0.47	5.5	100.0	19.6		0.09		23.2	0.11
United Kingdom	13 891	0.56	5.5	100.0	37.3	23.9	0.21	0.13	33.2	0.19
United States	30 687	0.19	4.6	100.0	17.0		0.03		37.2	0.07
Total DAC	126 949	0.29	2.0	94.6	30.2		0.09		31.9	0.09
Memo: Average country effoı		0.39								

Notes:

a. Excluding debt reorganisation.

b. Including EU institutions.

c. Excluding EU institutions.

.. Data not available.

Figure B.1 Net ODA from DAC countries in 2013

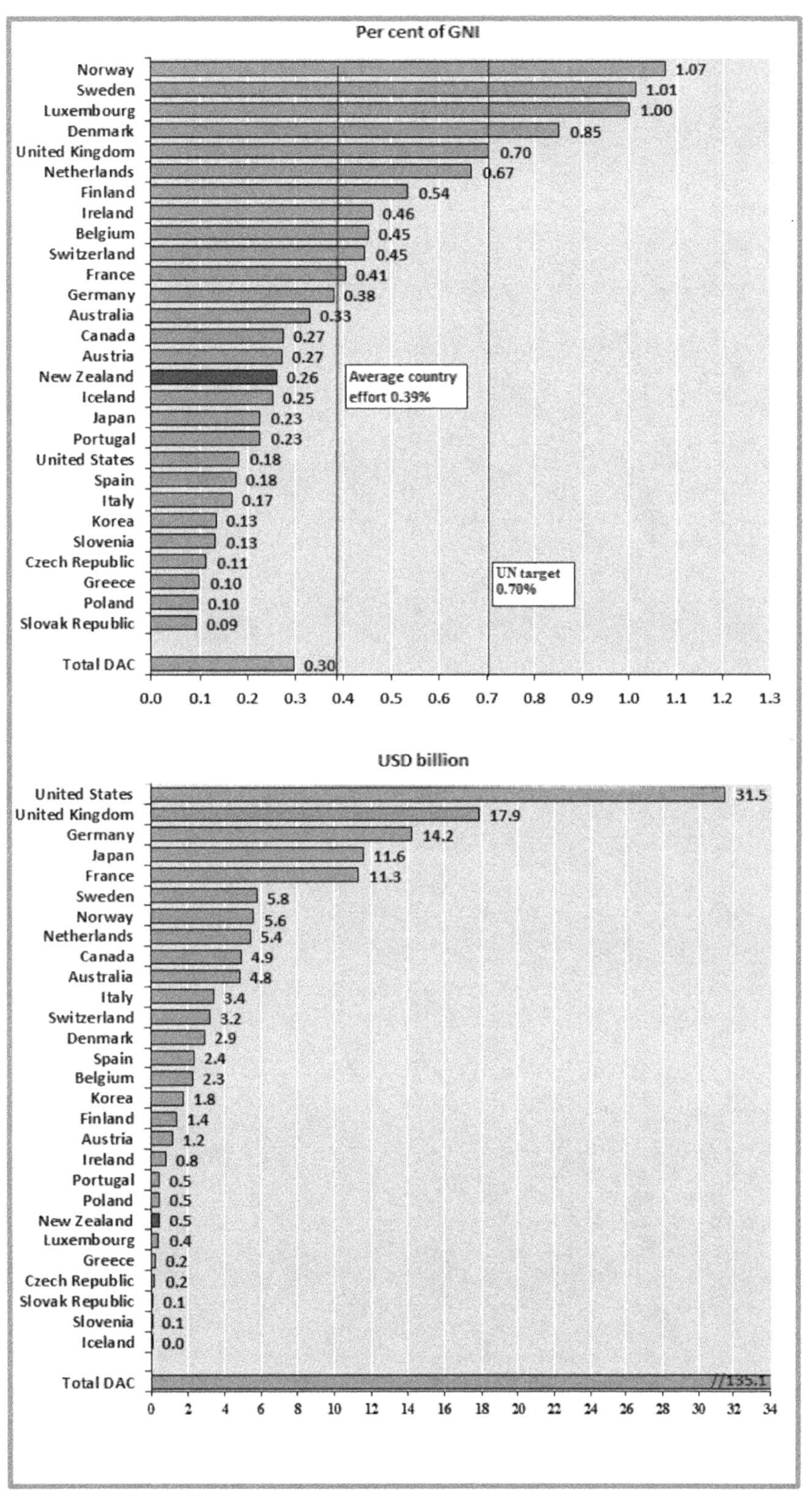

Annex C: Field visit to Kiribati

As part of the peer review of New Zealand, a team of examiners and the OECD secretariat visited Kiribati in November 2014. The team met with the High Commissioner, New Zealand development co-operation professionals, the President of Kiribati, partner country ministers and civil servants, other bilateral and multilateral partners, and representatives of partner country civil society organisations.

Kiribati faces unique development challenges

A country facing climate change, natural hazard, and social and economic challenges

The Independent and Sovereign Nation of Kiribati is an island nation in the central tropical Pacific Ocean. The permanent population is just over 100 000, spread over 800 square kilometres. The country comprises 32 atolls and one raised coral island, straddling the equator. It became independent from the United Kingdom in 1979, and since then has been a parliamentary republic. The official languages are English and Gilbertese.

Kiribati is expected to be the first country to lose almost all of its land territory to global climate change. In early 2012, the government purchased the 2 200 hectare Natoavatu Estate on Vanua Levu, Fiji,[1] to provide options for migration. In November 2013 President Tong began urging citizens to evacuate the islands and migrate elsewhere. Not surprisingly, therefore, Kiribati has been an active participant in international climate change discussions.

There is moderate risk of disasters, but even minor emergencies can overwhelm national capacity and the economy (RoK, 2012). Maritime disasters are a major risk, and long droughts can also occur, as can flooding. Kiribati is also located in an area of high seismic activity and is vulnerable to tsunami, tidal surges and sea level rise.

Kiribati is classified as a least developed country (LDC), but is expected to graduate from LDC status in the coming years. Kiribati is off-track on MDGs one, two, six and seven. It is rated "mixed" on MDGs three, four and five.[2]

Economically, Kiribati relies on copra and fishing, including renting out its waters to foreign fishing fleets. It also receives significant levels of remittances, and limited income from tourism. Most foodstuffs and manufactured items are imported; there is limited domestic production. There is a sovereign wealth fund from phosphate mining (phosphate reserves are now depleted), but it suffered during the financial crisis, and the IMF predicts that the fund will be depleted by 2030. The Australian dollar is used as currency. GNI per capita was USD 2 620 in 2013, with annual growth rates of around 3% (World Bank, n.d.). The current account deficit was 30.2% of GDP in 2013.

A small group of development partners

As Figure C.1 shows, there are few donors in Kiribati. Australia, Japan and New Zealand provided approximately 84% of gross ODA flowing in to Kiribati in 2013. In addition to these three, only IDA, the EU institutions and the Asian Development Bank Special Funds provided more than USD 1 million each (2012-13 average).

Figure C.1 Kiribati's aid at a glance

Kiribati

Receipts	2011	2012	2013
Net ODA (USD million)	64	65	64
Bilateral share (gross ODA)	91%	93%	75%
Net ODA / GNI	27.1%	25.0%	25.5%
Net Private flows (USD million)	3	0	0

For reference	2011	2012	2013
Population (million)	0.1	0.1	0.1
GNI per capita (Atlas USD)	2 100	2 520	2 620

Top Ten Donors of gross ODA (2012-13 average)		(USD m)
1	Australia	30
2	Japan	15
3	New Zealand	10
4	IDA	5
5	EU Institutions	3
6	AsDB Special Funds	2
7	WHO	1
8	GEF	0
9	Korea	0
10	GAVI	0

Bilateral ODA by Sector (2012-13)

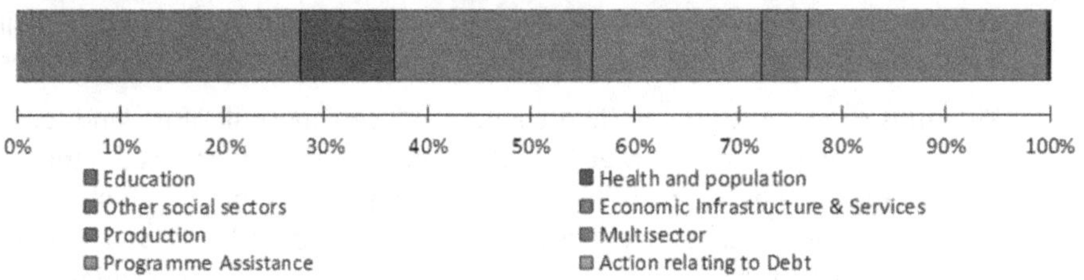

Sources: OECD - DAC, World Bank; www.oecd.org/dac/stats

New Zealand's development programme targets key areas of vulnerability

New Zealand's development co-operation with Kiribati focuses on (MFAT, 2014):

Lifting economic performance. Public (public financial management, improved infrastructure and key utilities including power supply). Private (improved economic performance, including increased fisheries, remittance and tourism income, and improved, safer, air and sea transport).

Promoting human development. Healthy population with less social and economic burden from population growth and disease. Skilled workforce better able to address economic and social challenges.

Urban water, sanitation and housing. Urban areas that promote social, economic and environmental well-being.

Partnerships. Strengthened partnerships that leverage New Zealand's private, non-government and public sector expertise.

The programme summary notes the challenges of working in Kiribati – low local human resource capability, limited operational budgets, extremely limited environment and economic constraints.

Forward Aid Plan (FAP) projections for total country aid flows (NZD):

- 2014/15 Forecast 26 220 921
- 2015/16 Forecast 17 173 906
- 2016/17 Forecast 14 657 501
- 2017/18 Forecast 12 931 409

New Zealand's policies, strategies and aid allocation

New Zealand is a valued partner in Kiribati

New Zealand's development co-operation in Kiribati is valued by both the Government of Kiribati, at the highest levels, and other development partners, as being flexible and pragmatic. It demonstrates a good understanding of the context and has built strong relationships.

Commitment to long-term engagement

New Zealand has a clear commitment to long-term engagement in Kiribati, fully recognising the nature of the challenges faced by a small Pacific nation with low capacity, few resources and severe climate risks. It is positive that New Zealand has recognised the primacy of the development relationship with Kiribati by appointing a high commissioner with a background in development support to Pacific island countries.

Upcoming country strategy paper is an opportunity for greater coherence across government

New Zealand is currently developing a long-term country strategy paper for Kiribati. The timeline for completion of this strategy is unclear, however it presents an opportunity for New Zealand to:

- demonstrate alignment with the Government of Kiribati's new development plan and present a consistent line of sight between New Zealand's strategy in Kiribati, the Joint Commitment for Development and the FAP
- present a clear whole-of-government strategy in line with the New Zealand Inc. approach, encompassing bilateral, regional, multilateral and other New Zealand government department priorities and results in Kiribati. This is important in Kiribati as a large share of the FAP is comprised of the non-bilateral programme
- clearly demonstrate how cross-cutting issues will be integrated and monitored across the programme, applying New Zealand strategies to the Kiribati context.

Poverty focus is not clear

Despite the policy commitments towards poverty reduction and reducing vulnerabilities, the Joint Commitment for Development does not clearly state how programmes in Kiribati will be selected, designed, implemented, monitored and evaluated with a poverty focus.

Organisation and management

Organisational changes not yet embedded in country offices

The re-integration of the International Development Group into the ministry could be further embedded in country offices. For example, New Zealand could clarify, and create certainty on, reporting lines and the direct accountability of IDG staff to heads of mission in particular.

More delegated authority would be useful

The programme would benefit from more delegated responsibility and authority to the country office, including in the space for design of the country strategy and programming. This would help ensure strategies and programmes are context specific, built on knowledge of local institutional constraints and risks, and draw on lessons from past experience.

Use of staff with specialist skills, including for capacity building, could be more systematic

It is not clear that New Zealand has the right skills in the right places. The use of technical specialists in Kiribati, such as that provided in the urban renewal portfolio, has helped accelerate and improve implementation. This could be made more systematic and longer term, with a stronger emphasis on capacity building of partners; lessons from this approach could be applied to other parts of the portfolio. Specialist skills are available to assist the programme from Wellington; however this appears to be insufficient to support ongoing analysis, dialogue and monitoring in key areas that should be part of every programme, including economics, social development and cross-cutting issues.

Partnerships, results and accountability

Good progress on effective development co-operation

New Zealand shows strong commitment to the principles of effective development co-operation in Kiribati. The programme is well aligned with government priorities; it is predictable, with medium-term spending plans; and New Zealand is part of an informal division of labour among the few development partners operating in Kiribati, while seeking opportunities to work jointly with other partners in sectors and programmes (e.g. health sector and scholarships programming). As the third largest provider of development assistance in Kiribati, New Zealand is showing good leadership and responsibility in supporting co-ordination among partners, in line with government priorities.

Use of budget support is good practice

The provision of budget support in Kiribati alongside the multilateral development banks, designed to incentivise and progress economic reforms, is a positive development. Budget support complements New Zealand's more targeted support to projects, and is indicative of an ongoing and welcome shift towards greater use of programme-based approaches across the bilateral portfolio. It is built upon a strong approach to assessing public financial management strengths and risks.

Box C.1 Development partner co-ordination in Kiribati

There are very few active development partners in Kiribati (Figure C.1). As a result, there is an appropriate division of labour. This is largely agreed on an informal basis between partners, and with government, in the absence of a Government of Kiribati aid management policy (PIF, 2014). In addition, the key partners, like Australia and New Zealand, are well harmonised and complementary in their approaches. For example, there are joint health sector reviews, joined up scholarship programmes, and harmonised budget support with the multilateral organisations. However, development partners with a staff presence in Kiribati report challenges in co-ordinating with those without a permanent staff presence.

Development Partner Forums with government are held every two years. Bilateral donors also tend to hold their own annual talks with government. However, at sector level, with the odd exception, working groups and co-ordination mechanisms do not operate effectively. Partners could do more to support government to revive these mechanisms, and reinforce government ownership and leadership (e.g. fewer projects and more programme-based approaches). Furthermore, the National Economic Planning Office in the Ministry of Finance has limited capacity, yet has to deal with increasing mission numbers (PIF, 2014).

The Kiribati Development Plan, 2016-2019, currently being developed, offers development partners an opportunity to reinforce ownership and alignment, reduce transaction costs for their government partner, and improve co-ordination.

Insufficient focus on capacity building	New Zealand is providing effective support to the implementation of projects and programmes in Kiribati. This includes some transfer of knowledge and skills, through technical assistance and other forms of support from across the New Zealand government. However, this does not yet represent a long-term strategy for building capacity in a low capacity environment. Given the recognition that New Zealand is likely to support Kiribati for many years to come, it could do more to build the capacity of government systems (including, for example, those related to statistical capacity), to complement the short-term output results being delivered through the programme.
Questions about the Partnerships Fund	The Partnerships for International Development Fund does not appear to be providing the right incentives for sustained engagement of New Zealand governmental and non-governmental partners in Kiribati. This is a missed opportunity to provide much needed ongoing technical support to reinforce the bilateral programme.
Further guidance needed on results	The Kiribati country programme lacks an overarching strategic results framework against which performance can be measured. Staff in the Kiribati country office, including local staff, have adopted a pragmatic approach to results at activity level, but would benefit from further guidance and training on results frameworks.
Evaluation not yet systematic	The Kiribati country office now appears to be using evaluation to generate learning and to inform new designs. However, there does not appear to be a clear plan, guided by the new evaluation policy and with input from the evaluation unit, as to how to select evaluations. This may compromise the use and value of evaluations from both a programming and corporate perspective.
Communication opportunities not being exploited	Kiribati is a good illustration of the development challenges in the Pacific, and there are positive stories about the impact of New Zealand's development co-operation over time. It is therefore a missed opportunity that communication materials are not being routinely requested or taken up from country programmes such as the one in Kiribati, to assist with raising development awareness and support in New Zealand.

Notes

1. See: www.ipsnews.net/2014/06/kiribati-president-purchases-worthless-resettlement-land-as-precaution-against-rising-sea.
2. See: www.un.org/millenniumgoals.

Bibliography

Government sources

MFAT (2014), *New Zealand – Kiribati Joint Commitment for Development*, agreement signed in Tarawa in April 2014, www.aid.govt.nz/sites/default/files/Kiribati%20JCfD%20April%202014.pdf.

Other sources

PIF (2014), *2014 Forum Compact Peer Review Countries Progress Report*, Fiji, Pacific Islands Forum Secretariat.

RoK (2012), *National Disaster Risk Management Plan*, Republic of Kiribati, Kiribati, http://reliefweb.int/report/kiribati/kiribati-national-disaster-risk-management-plan-october-2012.

World Bank (n.d.), "Kiribati", World Bank Data (dataset), http://data.worldbank.org/country/kiribati (accessed on 18 March 2015).

Annex D: Organisational structure

Chief Executive

Deputy Secretary Australia, Pacific, Europe Group	Deputy Secretary Americas and Asia, Middle East and Africa Group	Deputy Secretary Trade and Economic Group	Deputy Secretary Multilateral and Legal Affairs Group	**Deputy Secretary International Development Group**	Group Manager Services	Director Human Resources	Group Manager Strategy and Governance

International Development Group Structure

Deputy Secretary Office, IDG
(DS IDG)

Pacific Development Division (PACDEV)	**Global Development Division** (GLO)	**Partnerships, Humanitarian and Multilateral Division** (PHM)
• PNG, Solomons, Nauru • Kiribati, Vanuatu, Samoa • Fiji, Tuvalu, Tonga • Tokelau, Niue, Cook Islands	• Asia • Africa, Latin America and the Caribbean, Afghanistan, Timor Leste	• Humanitarian & Disaster Management • Multilateral & Pacific Regional • Partnership & Funds
Sustainable Economic Development Division (SED)	**Development, Strategy and Effectiveness Division** (DSE)	**Project and Activity Management Project** (PAM)
• Economic Development • Energy, Infrastructure & Environment • Human Development • Scholarships	• Development Effectiveness • Development Planning & Results • Evaluation & Research • Procurement and • Principal Development Manager, Policy	

ORGANISATION FOR ECONOMIC CO-OPERATION AND DEVELOPMENT

The OECD is a unique forum where governments work together to address the economic, social and environmental challenges of globalisation. The OECD is also at the forefront of efforts to understand and to help governments respond to new developments and concerns, such as corporate governance, the information economy and the challenges of an ageing population. The Organisation provides a setting where governments can compare policy experiences, seek answers to common problems, identify good practice and work to co-ordinate domestic and international policies.

The OECD member countries are: Australia, Austria, Belgium, Canada, Chile, the Czech Republic, Denmark, Estonia, Finland, France, Germany, Greece, Hungary, Iceland, Ireland, Israel, Italy, Japan, Korea, Luxembourg, Mexico, the Netherlands, New Zealand, Norway, Poland, Portugal, the Slovak Republic, Slovenia, Spain, Sweden, Switzerland, Turkey, the United Kingdom and the United States. The European Union takes part in the work of the OECD.

OECD Publishing disseminates widely the results of the Organisation's statistics gathering and research on economic, social and environmental issues, as well as the conventions, guidelines and standards agreed by its members.

DEVELOPMENT ASSISTANCE COMMITTEE

To achieve its aims, the OECD has set up a number of specialised committees. One of these is the Development Assistance Committee (DAC), whose mandate is to promote development co-operation and other policies so as to contribute to sustainable development - including pro-poor economic growth, poverty reduction and the improvement of living standards in developing countries - and to a future in which no country will depend on aid. To this end, the DAC has grouped the world's main donors, defining and monitoring global standards in key areas of development.

The members of the DAC are Australia, Austria, Belgium, Canada, the Czech Republic, Denmark, the European Union, Finland, France, Germany, Greece, Iceland, Ireland, Italy, Japan, Korea, Luxembourg, the Netherlands, New Zealand, Norway, Poland, Portugal, the Slovak Republic, Slovenia, Spain, Sweden, Switzerland, the United Kingdom and the United States.

The DAC issues guidelines and reference documents in the DAC Guidelines and Reference Series toinform and assist members in the conduct of their development co-operation programmes.

OECD PUBLISHING, 2, rue André-Pascal, 75775 PARIS CEDEX 16
(43 2015 06 1 P) ISBN 978-92-64-23557-1 – 2015

www.ingramcontent.com/pod-product-compliance
Lightning Source LLC
LaVergne TN
LVHW081416110826
845149LV00010B/1766